MW00887133

The DASH Diet Cookbook for Beginners

Essential Guide to Balanced Eating with Nutrient-Rich, Low-Sodium and High-Potassium Meals, Reduce Blood Pressure and Boost Wellness with a 28-Day Meal Prep Plan

By Jessica Fields

© Copyright 2023 by Jessica Fields - All rights reserved.
The following Book is reproduced below with the goal of providing information that is as accurate and reliable as possible. Regardless, purchasing this Book can be seen as consent to the fact that both the publisher and the author of this book are in no way experts on the topics discussed within and that any recommendations or suggestions that are made herein are for entertainment purposes only. Professionals should be consulted as needed prior to undertaking any of the action endorsed herein. This declaration is deemed fair and valid by both the American Bar Association and the Committee of Publishers Association and is legally binding throughout the United States. Furthermore, the transmission, duplication, or reproduction of any of the following work including specific information will be considered an illegal act irrespective of if it is done electronically or in print. This extends to creating a secondary or tertiary copy of the work or a recorded copy and is only allowed with the express written consent from the Publisher. All additional right reserved. The information in the following pages is broadly considered a truthful and accurate account of facts and as such, any inattention, use, or misuse of the information in question by the reader will render any resulting actions solely under their purview. There are no scenarios in which the publisher or the original author of this work can be in any fashion deemed liable for any hardship or damages that may befall them after undertaking information described herein. Additionally, the information in the following pages is intended only for informational purposes and should thus be thought of as universal. As befitting its nature, it is presented without assurance regarding its prolonged validity or interim quality. Trademarks that are mentioned are done without written consent and can in no way be considered an endorsement from the trademark holder

Introduction

In the vast landscape of dietary philosophies, the DASH Diet emerges as a beacon of hope for many. Its name, an acronym for "Dietary Approaches to Stop Hypertension," might sound clinical, but its essence is deeply rooted in the timeless principles of balanced and mindful eating. Let's embark on a journey to understand the philosophy behind this transformative diet.

A Return to Wholesomeness

At its core, the DASH Diet is not just about reducing hypertension, though that remains a significant benefit. It's a call to return to a more wholesome way of eating. In an era where processed foods and quick meals have become the norm, DASH beckons us to pause and reconsider. It reminds us of a time when meals were more than just fuel; they were moments of nourishment, both for the body and the soul.

The DASH Diet is a celebration of natural foods. It emphasizes fruits, vegetables, lean proteins, and whole grains. But more than the foods themselves, it's about the harmony they create when combined in the right proportions. It's a symphony of nutrients, where each ingredient plays a crucial role, and no single nutrient overshadows another.

The Power of Mindfulness

One of the most profound aspects of the DASH Diet is its emphasis on mindfulness. It's not just about what you eat but how you eat. The act of being present during meals, savoring each bite, and truly experiencing the flavors and textures can be transformative. This mindfulness extends beyond the dining table. It's about making conscious choices at the grocery store, understanding the origins of your food, and appreciating the journey it took to reach your plate.

This diet encourages us to form a deeper connection with our food. When we understand the impact of sodium on our bodies or recognize the benefits of potassium-rich foods, we're not just following guidelines; we're making informed decisions. It's this knowledge and awareness that empower us to make lasting changes.

A Holistic Approach to Health

While the primary focus of the DASH Diet is dietary, its philosophy encompasses a holistic view of health. It recognizes that food is just one piece of the puzzle. Physical activity, mental well-being, and emotional health are all intertwined. The DASH Diet, in its wisdom, doesn't isolate food from these factors but sees them as part of a larger, interconnected web.

For instance, consider stress, a common ailment in our fast-paced world. While the DASH Diet provides the nutrients to combat the physical manifestations of stress, such as hypertension, it also indirectly addresses the root causes. A meal rich in antioxidants, omega-3 fatty acids, and other essential nutrients can uplift one's mood, leading to a more positive outlook on life.

Embracing Flexibility

Another beautiful facet of the DASH philosophy is its flexibility. It's not a rigid set of rules but a guiding framework. It understands that every individual is unique, with their own set of challenges, preferences, and needs. Instead of imposing a one-size-fits-all approach, DASH provides the tools and knowledge for each person to carve their own path.

For some, this might mean a gradual reduction in sodium intake, while for others, it could be an exploration of new, nutrient-rich foods. The DASH Diet doesn't judge or dictate; it supports and guides.

The Health Benefits of the DASH Diet

The heart, often symbolized as the epicenter of emotion and vitality, is also a diligent organ that tirelessly pumps life through our veins. The DASH Diet, with its roots in combating hypertension, offers profound benefits for this vital organ. Hypertension, or high blood pressure, is frequently dubbed the "silent killer" because of its stealthy nature, often presenting no symptoms until it's too late. By emphasizing a reduction in sodium intake and promoting foods rich in potassium, calcium, and magnesium, the DASH Diet aids in regulating blood pressure, ensuring our heart functions optimally.

Beyond Blood Pressure: A Spectrum of Benefits

While the primary aim of the DASH Diet is to manage and prevent hypertension, its benefits cascade across various facets of our health. The emphasis on whole foods, rich in fiber and essential nutrients, aids in weight management. Shedding those extra pounds, even if it's a modest amount, can significantly reduce the risk of developing other chronic conditions like type 2 diabetes.

Moreover, the DASH Diet's rich palette of antioxidants, derived from fruits, vegetables, and grains, acts as a shield against oxidative stress. This not only slows down the aging process but also reduces the risk of several cancers.

Strengthening the Bones and Beyond

The focus on dairy products, especially those low in fat, ensures an adequate intake of calcium and vitamin D. These nutrients are paramount in maintaining bone health, reducing the risk of osteoporosis, especially in post-menopausal women. But the benefits don't stop at bones. Adequate calcium also plays a role in muscle function, nerve signaling, and ensuring our blood clots normally.

A Balm for the Mind

Our mental well-being is intricately tied to what we consume. The DASH Diet, rich in omega-3 fatty acids, B-vitamins, and antioxidants, offers a buffet of brain-boosting nutrients. Omega-3 fatty acids, found in fish and some plant sources, are known to reduce inflammation and are linked to a lower risk of chronic diseases. They also play a pivotal role in cognitive function, potentially delaying the onset of conditions like Alzheimer's.

Furthermore, the emphasis on whole grains, fruits, and vegetables ensures a steady release of glucose, the primary fuel for our brain. This not only aids in concentration but also stabilizes mood, reducing the risk of depression.

A Digestive Boon
The fiber-rich nature of the DASH Diet is a boon for our digestive system. Regular bowel movements, a reduction in the risk of colorectal cancer, and a thriving gut microbiome are just a few of the digestive benefits. A healthy gut, in turn, plays a role in everything from immunity to mental health.

How to Use This Book

As you turn the pages of this guide, it's essential to remember that adopting the DASH Diet is a journey, not a race. The beauty of this diet lies in its flexibility and adaptability, allowing it to be tailored to individual needs and preferences. This book is designed to be your companion on this journey, providing you with the knowledge, tools, and inspiration to make lasting changes.

A Tapestry of Knowledge and Practicality
While the subsequent chapters delve deep into the intricacies of the DASH Diet, from its history to its key nutritional principles, this book is more than just an informational guide. It's a blend of knowledge and practicality. Alongside the theoretical, you'll find tangible, actionable steps, from recipes to meal plans, ensuring that you can seamlessly integrate the DASH principles into your daily life.

Navigating the Chapters
Each chapter of this book has been meticulously crafted to offer a holistic view of the DASH Diet. However, you don't necessarily have to proceed linearly.
If you're eager to dive into the recipes, feel free to jump to the relevant chapters. If you're more interested in the science and rationale behind the diet, the initial chapters will satiate your curiosity.

Embracing Experimentation
The recipes provided are not set in stone but are rather templates. They're starting points, inviting you to experiment and tweak based on your preferences and dietary needs. Remember, the DASH Diet celebrates diversity and individuality. So, if a particular ingredient doesn't resonate with you, feel free to substitute or modify. The essence lies in the balance and nutrient profile, not rigid adherence to specific ingredients.

Seeking Support and Community
While this book is a comprehensive resource, the journey of adopting a new dietary lifestyle is enriched by community and support. Whether it's joining online forums, participating in local DASH Diet groups, or simply sharing your experiences with loved ones, remember that you're not alone on this journey. Sharing successes, challenges, and even recipes can make the process more enjoyable and sustainable.

Reflecting and Adapting

As you progress on your DASH journey, it's beneficial to periodically reflect on your experiences. What recipes have become your favorites? Are there any challenges you've faced? How do you feel, both physically and mentally? This reflection will not only provide insights but also allow you to adapt and evolve, ensuring that the DASH Diet remains a joyous and beneficial endeavor.

Chapter 1: Fundamentals of the DASH Diet

History and Origins of the DASH Diet

The latter half of the 20th century saw a sharp rise in lifestyle diseases, with hypertension leading the charge. As medical professionals grappled with this silent epidemic, it became evident that medication alone was not the solution. The need for a holistic approach, one that combined the power of nutrition with medicine, was palpable. And thus, in the corridors of research labs and the collaborative efforts of nutritionists, the DASH Diet was born.

The Pioneering Studies
The 1990s were pivotal in shaping the DASH narrative. Funded by the National Institutes of Health, a series of groundbreaking studies were initiated to explore the impact of dietary patterns on blood pressure. Researchers were not merely looking for individual superfoods but were keen on understanding the symphony of nutrients and how they interacted with each other.

In these studies, participants were divided into various groups, each following a different dietary pattern. One group adhered to a typical American diet, rich in processed foods and red meats. Another group was given a diet rich in fruits and vegetables but otherwise similar to the standard American diet. The third group followed what we now recognize as the DASH Diet: a balanced intake of fruits, vegetables, whole grains, lean proteins, and a reduced amount of red meat, sweets, and saturated fats.

The results were nothing short of revolutionary. While the group consuming more fruits and vegetables did see a reduction in their blood pressure, it was the DASH group that showcased the most significant improvements. This was a testament to the idea that while individual nutrient-rich foods have their benefits, it's the collective harmony of a well-balanced diet that holds transformative power.

Beyond Just a Diet: A Movement
The success of these studies propelled the DASH Diet from the confines of research labs to the broader public sphere. But its acceptance was not merely due to its efficacy. The DASH Diet resonated with many because it wasn't a restrictive regime. It didn't ask individuals to give up entire food groups or embark on drastic calorie reductions. Instead, it promoted balance, variety, and moderation.

Moreover, the DASH Diet was not just about hypertension. As more people adopted this dietary pattern, ancillary benefits began to emerge. Weight loss, improved heart health, and better glycemic control were just a few of the myriad advantages reported by DASH adherents.

What Does DASH Mean?

The choice of the word "Dietary" in the acronym is deliberate and poignant. It underscores the central tenet of the DASH philosophy: that food, in its myriad forms and combinations, can be a potent tool in managing and preventing high blood pressure. It shifts the focus from external interventions, like medication, to the choices we make on our plates every day. This emphasis on "approach" also speaks to the flexibility and adaptability of the DASH Diet. It's not a rigid set of rules but a guiding framework, a compass pointing towards healthier choices.

Stopping Hypertension: The Ultimate Goal

"Hypertension" might sound like a clinical term, but its implications are deeply personal. High blood pressure affects millions worldwide, often silently, leading to a range of complications from heart diseases to strokes. The word "Stop" in the acronym is a bold assertion. It's a commitment to halt the progression of this condition, to take proactive measures, and to reclaim control over one's health.

More Than Just Words: A Holistic Philosophy

While "Dietary Approaches to Stop Hypertension" succinctly captures the essence of the DASH Diet, the philosophy it embodies is expansive. It's not just about reducing salt or incorporating certain superfoods. DASH is a holistic approach to well-being.
It recognizes the interconnectedness of our body's systems and the symbiotic relationship between various nutrients. It's about balance, harmony, and the synergistic effect of making multiple beneficial dietary changes.

A Universal Resonance

One of the beauties of the DASH acronym is its universal resonance. Regardless of age, cultural background, or culinary preferences, the principles of DASH hold relevance. It's a testament to the universality of its message and the foundational nature of its guidelines.

Key Nutritional Principles of the DASH Diet

The DASH Diet is not about extremes. It doesn't advocate for a high-protein or low-carb approach. Instead, it seeks a harmonious balance between carbohydrates, proteins, and fats. Whole grains provide sustained energy, lean proteins aid in muscle repair and growth, and healthy fats support cellular function and heart health. This balanced approach ensures that the body receives a diverse array of nutrients, catering to its myriad functions.

Prioritizing Micronutrients

While macronutrients often grab the limelight, the DASH Diet places equal emphasis on micronutrients. Minerals like potassium, calcium, and magnesium are pivotal in the DASH narrative. These minerals play a crucial role in regulating blood pressure, with potassium, for instance, helping to counterbalance the effects of sodium.

Similarly, antioxidants derived from colorful fruits and vegetables combat oxidative stress, promoting cellular health and longevity.

Reducing Sodium, Not Eliminating It

A distinctive feature of the DASH Diet is its stance on sodium. Instead of advocating for its complete elimination, DASH promotes moderation. Sodium, in the right amounts, is vital for various bodily functions, including nerve signaling and muscle contraction. However, in excess, it can elevate blood pressure. The DASH Diet, therefore, encourages a mindful reduction, emphasizing natural sources of sodium over processed foods laden with added salts.

Celebrating Diversity and Variety

One of the joys of the DASH Diet is its celebration of food diversity. It doesn't pigeonhole individuals into consuming a narrow range of foods. From leafy greens and berries to fish and whole grains, the DASH plate is a mosaic of colors, textures, and flavors. This variety ensures a broad spectrum of nutrients while also catering to the palate's need for novelty and excitement.

Focusing on Whole Foods

In the DASH philosophy, the emphasis is on foods in their most natural state. Processed foods, with their additives, preservatives, and often hidden sugars and salts, are minimized. Instead, fresh fruits, vegetables, lean meats, and whole grains are championed. This focus on whole foods ensures that individuals receive nutrients without the baggage of unwanted additives.

The Benefits of Sodium Reduction

Sodium, a mineral often synonymous with table salt, plays a pivotal role in our body's physiological processes. From maintaining fluid balance to ensuring proper nerve transmission, its importance cannot be understated. However, like many things in life, it's all about balance. In the modern diet, where processed foods and dining out have become commonplace, sodium intake often surpasses recommended levels, leading to a cascade of health implications.

Blood Pressure and the Sodium Connection

One of the most immediate and well-documented effects of excessive sodium intake is its impact on blood pressure. Sodium has the ability to hold onto water, and when consumed in large quantities, it can lead to fluid retention.

This extra stored water raises blood pressure due to the added strain and pressure on the delicate blood vessels leading to the kidneys. Elevated blood pressure, or hypertension, is a significant risk factor for heart disease, stroke, and kidney disease, making sodium's influence far-reaching.

Beyond Blood Pressure: Other Health Impacts

While hypertension is a primary concern, the effects of excessive sodium don't stop there. High sodium intake has been linked to a higher risk of stomach cancer, exacerbated symptoms in individuals with asthma, and a strain on the kidneys as they work overtime to excrete the excess. Additionally, high sodium can lead to calcium excretion in the urine, which, over time, might impact bone density.

The DASH Diet's Stance on Sodium
The DASH Diet, rooted in scientific research and practical application, recognizes the need for sodium but emphasizes moderation. By focusing on whole foods and reducing reliance on processed items, sodium intake naturally decreases. The diet also champions foods rich in potassium, a mineral that counteracts some of sodium's effects on blood pressure, creating a harmonious balance.

The Tangible Benefits of Reduction
Reducing sodium intake, especially when combined with the holistic approach of the DASH Diet, can lead to tangible health benefits. Studies have shown that even a modest reduction in sodium can lead to significant drops in blood pressure, reducing the risk of cardiovascular events. Moreover, a lower sodium intake can alleviate the strain on the kidneys, promote better fluid balance, and potentially lead to better bone health.

A Lifestyle, Not a Restriction
It's essential to view sodium reduction not as a restriction but as a lifestyle choice. The DASH Diet doesn't advocate for the complete elimination of sodium; after all, it's a vital mineral.
Instead, it promotes awareness, mindfulness, and informed choices. By understanding the sources of high sodium and making conscious dietary swaps, individuals can enjoy flavorful meals without the health risks associated with excessive salt.

In Conclusion
The benefits of sodium reduction, especially within the framework of the DASH Diet, are profound. It's a testament to the idea that small, consistent changes can lead to significant health improvements. As we navigate the world of nutrition and health, understanding sodium's role and its influence on our well-being is paramount. The DASH Diet, with its balanced and informed approach, offers a roadmap to a healthier relationship with sodium and, by extension, a more vibrant life.

Chapter 2: Preparation for the DASH Diet

Kitchen Organization for the DASH Diet

The kitchen, often referred to as the heart of the home, plays a pivotal role in our dietary choices. It's where raw ingredients transform into nourishing meals, where culinary creativity flourishes, and where the principles of the DASH Diet come alive. But for this magic to happen consistently and efficiently, a well-organized kitchen is paramount.

The Power of Intentional Spaces
A kitchen tailored to the DASH Diet is more than just a space with pots and pans. It's an intentional space, designed to facilitate healthy choices and make the process of cooking not just convenient but enjoyable.

Zones of Purpose
Consider segmenting your kitchen into distinct zones based on function. Have a designated area for meal prep, complete with cutting boards, knives, and bowls. This zone should ideally be close to the refrigerator, allowing for easy access to fresh produce. Another zone could be dedicated to cooking, positioned near the stove and oven, stocked with essential pots, pans, and utensils. By creating these zones, you streamline the cooking process, making it intuitive and efficient.

The Visibility Factor
Out of sight often means out of mind. When embarking on the DASH Diet, it's beneficial to have healthy ingredients visible. Consider using clear storage containers for whole grains, nuts, and seeds. Not only does this make it easier to identify and access ingredients, but the visual reminder also reinforces healthy choices. Similarly, keep fresh fruits and vegetables at eye level in the refrigerator, making them the first thing you see when you open the door.

Tools of the Trade
The right tools can elevate the cooking experience, making it quicker and more efficient. For the DASH Diet, certain tools can be particularly beneficial.

The Importance of Measuring
Given the emphasis on sodium reduction and balanced nutrition, having a set of measuring cups and spoons is crucial. It ensures that you're using the right quantities, particularly for ingredients like salt or oil.

Versatile Appliances
Invest in appliances that align with the DASH principles. A good quality blender, for instance, can be used for smoothies, soups, and sauces. A slow cooker can help in creating delicious, low-sodium stews and curries.

An air fryer, as we'll explore in later chapters, can produce crispy delights without the excessive oil.

The Pantry Transformation
Your pantry can be a treasure trove of DASH-friendly ingredients, but it requires a bit of organization. Prioritize whole foods, stocking up on whole grains like quinoa, barley, and oats. Ensure you have a variety of herbs and spices; they'll be your allies in creating flavorful dishes without relying on salt. Processed foods, especially those high in sodium or added sugars, should be minimized or placed in less accessible spots.

Embracing Fluidity
While organization is key, it's also essential to embrace fluidity. Dietary needs and preferences evolve, and your kitchen should be adaptable to these changes. Periodically assess your kitchen setup, making tweaks based on your DASH journey's current phase.

Shopping List: Essential Foods for the DASH Diet

While water remains the gold standard for hydration, the beverages you choose can also contribute to your DASH Diet success.

Herbal Teas: Nature's Elixirs
Opt for herbal teas like chamomile, peppermint, or rooibos. They're caffeine-free and can be enjoyed hot or cold. These teas not only hydrate but also offer a range of antioxidants and other beneficial compounds.

Limiting Sugary Drinks
Sodas, sweetened teas, and some fruit juices can be high in added sugars, which can contribute to weight gain and other health issues. Instead, flavor your water with slices of fresh fruit, cucumber, or herbs for a refreshing twist.

Snacking Smart: Mindful Munchies
Snacks can be a part of a balanced DASH Diet, but it's crucial to choose wisely.

Nuts and Seeds: Crunchy Nutrients
Almonds, walnuts, chia seeds, and flaxseeds are nutrient powerhouses. They provide healthy fats, protein, and fiber. However, moderation is key due to their calorie density.

Fresh Fruits: Nature's Candy
Instead of reaching for sugary snacks, let fresh fruits satisfy your sweet cravings. Apples, berries, oranges, and pears are portable and packed with vitamins and fiber.

Reading Labels: An Empowered Shopper's Tool
As you fill your cart with DASH-friendly foods, it's essential to become proficient in reading nutrition labels.

Sodium Watch
Always check the sodium content, especially in packaged foods. Even products that don't taste salty can have hidden sodium. Opt for low-sodium or sodium-free versions when available.

Checking Sugars and Fats
Look out for added sugars, which can lurk under various names like high fructose corn syrup or cane juice. Also, check the type of fats used, prioritizing products with unsaturated fats and avoiding those with trans fats.

Shopping Outside the Box: Local and Seasonal
While supermarkets offer convenience, consider exploring local farmers' markets. They often provide fresh, seasonal produce that supports local farmers and can be richer in nutrients due to reduced transport time.

Planning Ahead: A Shopper's Best Friend
Before heading to the store, plan your meals for the week. This not only ensures you buy all the necessary ingredients but also reduces the chances of impulse purchases that might not align with the DASH principles.

Tips for Eating Out on the DASH Diet

Before heading to a restaurant, take a few mins to browse their menu online. Many establishments provide nutritional information, allowing you to make informed choices. If not, a quick glance can still give you an idea of DASH-friendly options.

Communication is Key: Speak to Your Server
Don't hesitate to ask questions. Whether it's about the ingredients, preparation method, or portion sizes, your server can provide valuable insights. Express your dietary preferences clearly. Most restaurants are accommodating and can make minor tweaks to dishes to align them with the DASH principles.

Opt for Grilled, Steamed, or Baked
When scanning the menu, look for keywords that indicate healthier preparation methods. Grilled fish, steamed vegetables, or baked chicken are typically lower in added fats and sodium compared to their fried or creamy counterparts.

Beware of the Salt Shaker
While it's tempting to season your food further, remember that restaurant dishes often already contain significant amounts of sodium. Taste your food first before reaching for the salt shaker.

Mind the Portions: Less Can Be More
Restaurant portions can be generous, often exceeding standard serving sizes. Consider sharing a dish with a dining companion or ask for a half portion. Alternatively, you can request a takeout box right away and save half for another meal.

Choose Beverages Wisely
Sugary sodas, cocktails, and some fruit juices can add unnecessary Cal and sugar to your meal. Opt for water, herbal teas, or unsweetened beverages. If you're having alcohol, choose wine or a light beer and always drink in moderation.

Salads: A Double-Edged Sword
While salads can be a nutritious choice, be wary of dressings and toppings.
Creamy dressings, croutons, and certain cheeses can quickly elevate the calorie, fat, and sodium content. Opt for vinaigrettes on the side, allowing you to control the amount.

Desserts: Savor in Moderation
If you have a sweet tooth, choose fruit-based desserts or share a richer dessert with a friend. Savor each bite, focusing on the flavors and textures, which can enhance satisfaction and reduce the urge to overindulge.

Reflect and Learn
After dining out, take a moment to reflect on your choices. Were there dishes that aligned well with the DASH principles? Were there challenges? Each dining experience offers a learning opportunity, helping you make even better choices in the future.

Chapter 3: Recipes for Breakfast

Grains and Cereals

Quinoa and Berry Breakfast Bowl

PREP: 10 mins
Cook T.: 15 mins
Serves: 2
Ingr:
- 1 C cooked quinoa
- 1/2 C mixed berries (blueberries, raspberries, strawberries)
- 1 tbsp chia seeds
- 1 C almond milk
- 1 tbsp honey

Proc:
1. Cook quinoa according to package instructions.
2. In a bowl, mix cooked quinoa with almond milk.
3. Top with mixed berries.
4. Sprinkle chia seeds over the top.
5. Drizzle with honey and serve.

Nutritional Values: Cal: 220, Protein: 8g, Carbs: 40g, Fat: 5g, Sodium: 10mg, Fiber: 5g

Oatmeal with Cinnamon and Apple

PREP: 5 mins
Cook T.: 10 mins
Serves: 2
Ingr:
- 1 C rolled oats
- 1 apple, diced
- 1/2 tsp cinnamon
- 2 Cs water
- 1 tbsp maple syrup

Proc:
1. Bring water to a boil in a pot.
2. Add rolled oats and simmer for 10 mins.
3. Stir in diced apple and cinnamon.
4. Cook for an additional 2 mins.
5. Serve in bowls and drizzle with maple syrup.

Nutritional Values: Cal: 210, Protein: 6g, Carbs: 45g, Fat: 3g, Sodium: 15mg, Fiber: 6g

Millet Porridge with Banana

PREP: 5 mins
Cook T.: 20 mins
Serves: 2
Ingr:
- 1 C millet
- 2 Cs water
- 1 banana, sliced
- 1 tbsp almond butter
- 1/2 tsp vanilla extract

Proc:
1. Rinse millet under cold water.
2. In a pot, bring water to a boil and add millet.
3. Simmer for 20 mins until millet is soft.
4. Stir in vanilla extract.

5. Serve in bowls, top with sliced banana and a drizzle of almond butter.

Nutritional Values: Cal: 230, Protein: 7g, Carbs: 48g, Fat: 4g, Sodium: 10mg, Fiber: 4g

Barley and Nut Breakfast Pudding

PREP: 10 mins
Cook T.: 40 mins
Serves: 2
Ingr:
- 1 C pearled barley
- 2 Cs water
- 1/4 C mixed nuts (almonds, walnuts, pecans)
- 1 tbsp honey
- 1/2 tsp ground nutmeg

Proc:
1. Rinse barley under cold water.
2. In a pot, bring water to a boil and add barley.
3. Simmer for 40 mins until barley is tender.
4. Stir in ground nutmeg.
5. Serve in bowls, top with mixed nuts and drizzle with honey.

Nutritional Values: Cal: 240, Protein: 8g, Carbs: 50g, Fat: 5g, Sodium: 20mg, Fiber: 7g

Rye Flakes and Dried Fruit Compote

PREP: 5 mins
Cook T.: 10 mins
Serves: 2
Ingr:
- 1 C rye flakes
- 2 Cs water
- 1/4 C mixed dried fruits (raisins, apricots, cranberries)
- 1 tbsp coconut flakes
- 1/2 tsp ground cloves

Proc:
1. Bring water to a boil in a pot.
2. Add rye flakes and simmer for 10 mins.
3. Stir in ground cloves.
4. Serve in bowls, top with dried fruits and sprinkle with coconut flakes.

Nutritional Values: Cal: 200, Protein: 6g, Carbs: 42g, Fat: 3g, Sodium: 15mg, Fiber: 5g

Buckwheat and Berry Morning Delight

PREP: 5 mins
Cook T.: 15 mins
Serves: 2
Ingr:
- 1 C buckwheat groats
- 2 Cs water
- 1/2 C fresh berries (blueberries, raspberries)
- 1 tbsp agave syrup
- 1/2 tsp ground cardamom

Proc:
1. Rinse buckwheat under cold water.
2. In a pot, bring water to a boil and add buckwheat.
3. Simmer for 15 mins until tender.
4. Stir in ground cardamom.
5. Serve in bowls, top with fresh berries and drizzle with agave syrup.

Nutritional Values: Cal: 210, Protein: 7g, Carbs: 44g, Fat: 2g, Sodium: 10mg, Fiber: 4g

Whole Wheat Berry Pancakes

PREP: 10 mins
Cook T.: 15 mins
Serves: 4
Ingr:
- 1 C whole wheat flour
- 1/2 C mixed berries (blueberries, strawberries, raspberries)
- 1 C almond milk
- 1 tsp baking powder
- 1 tbsp honey

Proc:
1. In a bowl, mix whole wheat flour and baking powder.
2. Gradually add almond milk to form a batter.
3. Heat a non-stick skillet and pour a ladle of batter.
4. Sprinkle some berries on top.
5. Flip when bubbles appear and cook until golden brown. Serve with honey.

Nutritional Values: Cal: 180, Protein: 5g, Carbs: 38g, Fat: 2g, Sodium: 80mg, Fiber: 6g

Cornmeal and Apple Porridge

PREP: 5 mins
Cook T.: 20 mins
Serves: 2
Ingr:
- 1 C cornmeal
- 2 Cs water
- 1 apple, diced
- 1 tbsp maple syrup
- 1/2 tsp cinnamon

Proc:
1. Bring water to a boil in a pot.
2. Gradually whisk in cornmeal to avoid lumps.
3. Add diced apple and cinnamon.
4. Simmer until thickened. Serve with maple syrup.

Nutritional Values: Cal: 220, Protein: 4g, Carbs: 48g, Fat: 2g, Sodium: 10mg, Fiber: 5g

Spelt and Nut Muesli

PREP: 10 mins
Cook T.: 0 mins
Serves: 2
Ingr:
- 1 C spelt flakes
- 1/4 C mixed nuts (almonds, walnuts, hazelnuts)
- 1 C yogurt
- 1 tbsp honey
- 1/2 tsp vanilla extract

Proc:
1. In a bowl, mix spelt flakes and mixed nuts.
2. Add yogurt, honey, and vanilla extract.
3. Stir well and serve chilled.

Nutritional Values: Cal: 230, Protein: 8g, Carbs: 35g, Fat: 8g, Sodium: 40mg, Fiber: 6g

Amaranth and Coconut Bowl

PREP: 5 mins
Cook T.: 20 mins
Serves: 2
Ingr:
- 1 C amaranth
- 2 Cs coconut milk
- 1 tbsp shredded coconut
- 1 tbsp agave syrup
- 1/2 tsp cardamom

Proc:
1. In a pot, bring coconut milk to a boil.
2. Add amaranth and simmer until soft.
3. Stir in cardamom. Serve topped with shredded coconut and agave syrup.

Nutritional Values: Cal: 240, Protein: 7g, Carbs: 40g, Fat: 8g, Sodium: 15mg, Fiber: 5g

Sorghum and Date Pudding

PREP: 10 mins
Cook T.: 30 mins
Serves: 2
Ingr:
- 1 C sorghum
- 2 Cs water
- 4 dates, pitted and chpd
- 1 tbsp almond butter
- 1/2 tsp nutmeg

Proc:
1. Rinse sorghum under cold water.
2. In a pot, bring water to a boil and add sorghum.
3. Simmer until tender.
4. Stir in dates and nutmeg. Serve with a dollop of almond butter.

Nutritional Values: Cal: 210, Protein: 6g, Carbs: 45g, Fat: 4g, Sodium: 10mg, Fiber: 6g

Teff and Cinnamon Porridge

PREP: 5 mins
Cook T.: 15 mins
Serves: 2
Ingr:
- 1 C teff
- 2 Cs almond milk
- 1 tbsp raisins
- 1 tbsp honey
- 1/2 tsp cinnamon

Proc:
1. In a pot, bring almond milk to a boil.
2. Add teff and simmer until soft.
3. Stir in cinnamon. Serve topped with raisins and honey.

Nutritional Values: Cal: 220, Protein: 7g, Carbs: 40g, Fat: 3g, Sodium: 20mg, Fiber: 6g

Egg-Based Dishes

Spinach and Feta Omelette

PREP: 5 mins
Cook T.: 10 mins
Serves: 1
Ingr:
- 2 eggs
- 1/4 C spinach, chpd
- 1/4 C feta cheese, crumbled
- 1 tsp olive oil
- S/P to taste

Proc:

1. Whisk eggs in a bowl.
2. Heat olive oil in a non-stick skillet.
3. Add spinach and sauté until wilted.
4. Pour in eggs and sprinkle feta on top.
5. Cook until set, fold, and serve.

Nutritional Values: Cal: 220, Protein: 14g, Carbs: 2g, Fat: 17g, Sodium: 320mg, Fiber: 0.5g

Mushroom and Chive Scramble

PREP: 5 mins
Cook T.: 10 mins
Serves: 1
Ingr:
- 2 eggs
- 1/4 C mushrooms, sliced
- 1 tbsp chives, chpd
- 1 tsp olive oil
- S/P to taste

Proc:

1. Whisk eggs in a bowl.
2. Heat olive oil in a skillet.
3. Add mushrooms and sauté until browned.
4. Add eggs and chives, scramble until cooked.

Nutritional Values: Cal: 180, Protein: 12g, Carbs: 3g, Fat: 13g, Sodium: 210mg, Fiber: 0.8g

Tomato and Basil Frittata

PREP: 10 mins
Cook T.: 15 mins
Serves: 2
Ingr:
- 4 eggs
- 1 tomato, sliced
- 1/4 C fresh basil, chpd
- 1 tsp olive oil
- S/P to taste

Proc:

1. Preheat oven to 375°F (190°C).
2. Whisk eggs in a bowl.
3. Heat olive oil in an oven-safe skillet.
4. Add tomatoes and basil, sauté briefly.
5. Pour in eggs, cook until edges set.
6. Transfer skillet to oven, bake until center sets.

Nutritional Values: Cal: 210, Protein: 14g, Carbs: 4g, Fat: 15g, Sodium: 220mg, Fiber: 1g

Zucchini and Parmesan Fluffy Omelette

PREP: 5 mins
Cook T.: 10 mins
Serves: 1
Ingr:
- 2 eggs
- 1/4 C zucchini, grated
- 2 tbsp Parmesan cheese, grated
- 1 tsp olive oil
- S/P to taste

Proc:
1. Whisk eggs until frothy.
2. Heat olive oil in a skillet.
3. Add zucchini and sauté until softened.
4. Pour in eggs, sprinkle Parmesan on top.
5. Cook until set, fold, and serve.

Nutritional Values: Cal: 230, Protein: 16g, Carbs: 3g, Fat: 17g, Sodium: 340mg, Fiber: 0.7g

Bell Pepper and Onion Mini Quiches

PREP: 10 mins
Cook T.: 20 mins
Serves: 4
Ingr:
- 4 eggs
- 1/4 C bell pepper, diced
- 1/4 C onion, diced
- 1/4 C milk
- S/P to taste

Proc:
1. Preheat oven to 375°F (190°C).
2. Whisk eggs and milk in a bowl.
3. Add bell pepper and onion.
4. Pour mixture into greased muffin tins.
5. Bake until set and golden.

Nutritional Values: Cal: 110, Protein: 8g, Carbs: 4g, Fat: 7g, Sodium: 180mg, Fiber: 0.6g

Asparagus and Goat Cheese Frittata

PREP: 10 mins
Cook T.: 15 mins
Serves: 2
Ingr:
- 4 eggs
- 1/4 C asparagus, chpd
- 1/4 C goat cheese, crumbled
- 1 tsp olive oil
- S/P to taste

Proc:
1. Preheat oven to 375°F (190°C).
2. Whisk eggs in a bowl.
3. Heat olive oil in an oven-safe skillet.
4. Add asparagus and sauté until tender.
5. Pour in eggs, sprinkle goat cheese on top.
6. Transfer skillet to oven, bake until set.

Nutritional Values: Cal: 220, Protein: 16g, Carbs: 3g, Fat: 16g, Sodium: 290mg, Fiber: 1g

Kale and Garlic Poached Eggs

PREP: 5 mins
Cook T.: 10 mins
Serves: 1
Ingr:
- 2 eggs
- 1/4 C kale, chpd
- 1 garlic clove, minced
- 1 tsp olive oil
- 2 Cs water

Proc:

1. Heat olive oil in a skillet.
2. Add kale and garlic, sauté until wilted.
3. In a pot, bring water to a simmer.
4. Crack eggs into water, poach until whites set.
5. Serve eggs over kale.

Nutritional Values: Cal: 190, Protein: 14g, Carbs: 4g, Fat: 13g, Sodium: 210mg, Fiber: 1.2g

Broccoli and Cheddar Breakfast Muffins

PREP: 10 mins
Cook T.: 20 mins
Serves: 4
Ingr:
- 4 eggs
- 1/4 C broccoli, chpd
- 1/4 C cheddar cheese, grated
- 1/4 C milk
- S/P to taste

Proc:

1. Preheat oven to 375°F (190°C).
2. Whisk eggs and milk in a bowl.
3. Add broccoli and cheddar.
4. Pour mixture into greased muffin tins.
5. Bake until set and golden.

Nutritional Values: Cal: 150, Protein: 11g, Carbs: 3g, Fat: 10g, Sodium: 250mg, Fiber: 0.8g

Spinach and Tomato Egg Muffins

PREP: 10 mins
Cook T.: 20 mins
Serves: 4
Ingr:
- 4 eggs
- 1/4 C spinach, chpd
- 1/4 C tomatoes, diced
- 1/4 C milk
- S/P to taste

Proc:

1. Preheat oven to 375°F (190°C).
2. Whisk eggs and milk in a bowl.
3. Add spinach and tomatoes.
4. Pour mixture into greased muffin tins.
5. Bake until set and golden.

Nutritional Values: Cal: 120, Protein: 9g, Carbs: 3g, Fat: 8g, Sodium: 190mg, Fiber: 0.9g

Avocado and Egg Breakfast Bowl

PREP: 5 mins
Cook T.: 10 mins
Serves: 1
Ingr:
- 2 eggs
- 1/2 avocado, sliced
- 1 tsp olive oil
- S/P to taste
- 1 tbsp chives, chpd

Proc:

1. Heat olive oil in a skillet.
2. Crack eggs into skillet, cook to desired doneness.
3. Place eggs in a bowl, surround with avocado slices.
4. Sprinkle with chives, salt, and pepper.

Nutritional Values: Cal: 280, Protein: 14g, Carbs: 8g, Fat: 23g, Sodium: 210mg, Fiber: 6g

Herb and Egg Breakfast Wrap

PREP: 5 mins
Cook T.: 10 mins
Serves: 1
Ingr:

- 2 eggs
- 1 whole wheat tortilla
- 1 tbsp mixed herbs (parsley, cilantro, dill), chpd
- 1 tsp olive oil
- S/P to taste

Proc:

1. Whisk eggs and herbs in a bowl.
2. Heat olive oil in a skillet.
3. Pour in egg mixture, scramble until cooked.
4. Place scrambled eggs in the center of the tortilla, fold, and serve.

Nutritional Values: Cal: 230, Protein: 12g, Carbs: 20g, Fat: 12g, Sodium: 310mg, Fiber: 3g

Sundried Tomato and Mozzarella Egg Cs

PREP: 10 mins
Cook T.: 20 mins
Serves: 4
Ingr:

- 4 eggs
- 1/4 C sundried tomatoes, chpd
- 1/4 C mozzarella cheese, shredded
- 1/4 C fresh basil, chpd
- S/P to taste

Proc:

1. Preheat oven to 375°F (190°C).
2. In a bowl, whisk together eggs, salt, and pepper.
3. Stir in sundried tomatoes, mozzarella cheese, and half of the basil.
4. Pour the mixture into greased muffin tins.
5. Bake for 18-20 mins or until the centers are set.
6. Garnish with the remaining fresh basil before serving.

Nutritional Values: Cal: 160, Protein: 11g, Carbs: 5g, Fat: 11g, Sodium: 220mg, Fiber: 1g

Smoothies and Drinks

Berry Bliss Smoothie

PREP: 5 mins
Cook T.: 0 mins
Serves: 1
Ingr:
- 1/2 C mixed berries (blueberries, raspberries, strawberries)
- 1 C almond milk
- 1 tbsp chia seeds
- 1 tsp honey
- 1/2 banana

Proc:
1. Combine all ingredients in a blender.
2. Blend until smooth.
3. Pour into a glass and serve immediately.

Nutritional Values: Cal: 180, Protein: 4g, Carbs: 30g, Fat: 6g, Sodium: 150mg, Fiber: 8g

Tropical Morning Smoothie

PREP: 5 mins
Cook T.: 0 mins
Serves: 1
Ingr:
- 1/2 C pineapple chunks
- 1/2 C mango chunks
- 1 C coconut water
- 1 tbsp flaxseeds
- 1/2 tsp turmeric

Proc:
1. Place all ingredients in a blender.
2. Blend until creamy and smooth.
3. Serve in a tall glass with a slice of pineapple on the rim.

Nutritional Values: Cal: 150, Protein: 2g, Carbs: 32g, Fat: 3g, Sodium: 60mg, Fiber: 5g

Green Goddess Smoothie

PREP: 5 mins
Cook T.: 0 mins
Serves: 1
Ingr:
- 1 C spinach
- 1/2 avocado
- 1 C water
- 1 tbsp lemon juice
- 1 tsp ginger, grated

Proc:
1. Combine all ingredients in a blender.
2. Blend until velvety and even.
3. Pour into a glass and enjoy.

Nutritional Values: Cal: 140, Protein: 2g, Carbs: 10g, Fat: 11g, Sodium: 25mg, Fiber: 6g

Banana Oat Boost

PREP: 5 mins
Cook T.: 0 mins
Serves: 1
Ingr:
- 1 banana
- 1/4 C oats
- 1 C almond milk
- 1 tbsp almond butter
- 1/2 tsp cinnamon

Proc:
1. Add all ingredients to a blender.
2. Blend until smooth and creamy.
3. Serve in a glass with a sprinkle of cinnamon on top.

Nutritional Values: Cal: 280, Protein: 7g, Carbs: 40g, Fat: 12g, Sodium: 150mg, Fiber: 7g

Choco-Peanut Delight

PREP: 5 mins
Cook T.: 0 mins
Serves: 1
Ingr:
- 1 tbsp cocoa powder
- 1 tbsp peanut butter
- 1 C almond milk
- 1 banana
- 1 tsp honey

Proc:
1. Place all ingredients in a blender.
2. Blend until smooth and rich.
3. Pour into a glass and savor the creamy texture.

Nutritional Values: Cal: 290, Protein: 8g, Carbs: 35g, Fat: 15g, Sodium: 180mg, Fiber: 6g

Refreshing Cucumber Mint Drink

PREP: 5 mins
Cook T.: 0 mins
Serves: 1
Ingr:
- 1 cucumber, peeled and sliced
- 1 C water
- 1 tbsp mint leaves
- 1 tsp lemon juice
- 1 tsp honey

Proc:
1. Combine cucumber, mint leaves, and water in a blender.
2. Blend until smooth.
3. Strain the mixture into a glass.
4. Add lemon juice and honey, stir well.

Nutritional Values: Cal: 40, Protein: 1g, Carbs: 10g, Fat: 0.5g, Sodium: 10mg, Fiber: 1g

Golden Turmeric Latte

PREP: 5 mins
Cook T.: 5 mins
Serves: 1
Ingr:
- 1 C almond milk
- 1 tsp turmeric powder
- 1/2 tsp ginger, grated
- 1 tsp honey
- A pinch of black pepper

Proc:
1. Heat almond milk in a saucepan.
2. Add turmeric, ginger, and black pepper.
3. Simmer for 5 mins.

4. Pour into a mug, stir in honey, and enjoy.

Nutritional Values: Cal: 70, Protein: 1g, Carbs: 10g, Fat: 3g, Sodium: 150mg, Fiber: 1g

Strawberry Almond Bliss

PREP: 5 mins
Cook T.: 0 mins
Serves: 1
Ingr:
- 1/2 C strawberries
- 1 C almond milk
- 1 tbsp almond butter
- 1 tsp chia seeds
- 1 tsp honey

Proc:
1. Combine all ingredients in a blender.
2. Blend until smooth and creamy.
3. Pour into a glass and garnish with a strawberry slice.

Nutritional Values: Cal: 220, Protein: 6g, Carbs: 20g, Fat: 14g, Sodium: 150mg, Fiber: 6g

Blueberry Lavender Smoothie

PREP: 5 mins
Cook T.: 0 mins
Serves: 1
Ingr:
- 1/2 C blueberries
- 1 C almond milk
- 1 tsp dried lavender
- 1 tbsp honey
- 1/2 banana

Proc:
1. Combine all ingredients in a blender.
2. Blend until smooth and velvety.
3. Pour into a glass and enjoy the calming flavors.

Nutritional Values: Cal: 180, Protein: 3g, Carbs: 30g, Fat: 6g, Sodium: 150mg, Fiber: 4g

Peachy Keen Smoothie

PREP: 5 mins
Cook T.: 0 mins
Serves: 1
Ingr:
- 1 peach, sliced
- 1 C almond milk
- 1 tbsp flaxseeds
- 1 tsp honey
- 1/2 tsp vanilla extract

Proc:
1. Add all ingredients to a blender.
2. Blend until creamy and smooth.
3. Serve in a tall glass with a slice of peach on the rim.

Nutritional Values: Cal: 170, Protein: 4g, Carbs: 25g, Fat: 7g, Sodium: 150mg, Fiber: 5g

Zesty Orange and Carrot Smoothie

PREP: 5 mins
Cook T.: 0 mins
Serves: 1
Ingr:
- 1 orange, peeled and segmented
- 1 carrot, peeled and chpd
- 1 C almond milk
- 1 tsp honey
- 1/2 tsp grated ginger

Proc:
1. Place all ingredients in a blender.
2. Blend until smooth and vibrant.
3. Pour into a glass, garnish with a slice of orange, and enjoy the zesty kick.

Nutritional Values: Cal: 160, Protein: 3g, Carbs: 30g, Fat: 4g, Sodium: 150mg, Fiber: 5g

Kiwi and Spinach Detox Drink

PREP: 5 mins
Cook T.: 0 mins
Serves: 1
Ingr:
- 2 kiwis, peeled and sliced
- 1 C spinach leaves
- 1 C water
- 1 tbsp lemon juice
- 1 tsp chia seeds

Proc:
1. Combine kiwis, spinach, water, and lemon juice in a blender.
2. Blend until smooth and even.
3. Pour into a glass, sprinkle chia seeds on top, and stir gently.

Nutritional Values: Cal: 120, Protein: 4g, Carbs: 25g, Fat: 2g, Sodium: 20mg, Fiber: 6g

Chapter 4: Recipes for Lunch

Salads

Mediterranean Chickpea Salad

PREP: 10 mins
Cook T.: 0 mins
Serves: 2
Ingr:

- 1 C chickpeas, cooked and drained
- 1/2 C cherry tomatoes, halved
- 1/4 C cucumber, diced
- 1/4 C feta cheese, crumbled
- 2 tbsp olive oil

Proc:

1. In a large bowl, combine chickpeas, cherry tomatoes, and cucumber.
2. Drizzle with olive oil and toss gently to coat.
3. Sprinkle with crumbled feta cheese.
4. Season with S/P to taste.
5. Serve chilled.

Nutritional Values: Cal: 250, Protein: 8g, Carbs: 25g, Fat: 14g, Sodium: 250mg, Fiber: 6g

---

Spinach and Strawberry Salad

PREP: 10 mins
Cook T.: 0 mins
Serves: 2
Ingr:

- 2 Cs fresh spinach leaves
- 1 C strawberries, sliced
- 1/4 C walnuts, chpd
- 1/4 C goat cheese, crumbled
- 2 tbsp balsamic vinaigrette

Proc:

1. Place spinach leaves in a large bowl.
2. Top with sliced strawberries and chpd walnuts.
3. Drizzle with balsamic vinaigrette.
4. Sprinkle with crumbled goat cheese.
5. Toss gently and serve immediately.

Nutritional Values: Cal: 180, Protein: 6g, Carbs: 12g, Fat: 12g, Sodium: 180mg, Fiber: 3g

---

Quinoa and Avocado Bowl

PREP: 15 mins
Cook T.: 20 mins
Serves: 2
Ingr:

- 1 C quinoa, cooked
- 1 avocado, sliced
- 1/2 C bell peppers, diced
- 1/4 C red onion, finely chpd
- 2 tbsp lemon juice

Proc:

1. In a large bowl, mix cooked quinoa, bell peppers, and red onion.
2. Drizzle with lemon juice and toss to combine.
3. Top with avocado slices.
4. Season with S/P to taste.
5. Serve at room temperature or chilled.

Nutritional Values: Cal: 320, Protein: 8g, Carbs: 45g, Fat: 14g, Sodium: 10mg, Fiber: 8g

Roasted Beet and Arugula Salad

PREP: 10 mins
Cook T.: 25 mins
Serves: 2
Ingr:

- 2 medium beets, roasted and sliced
- 2 Cs arugula
- 1/4 C goat cheese, crumbled
- 2 tbsp walnuts, toasted
- 2 tbsp olive oil

Proc:

1. Place arugula in a large salad bowl.
2. Top with roasted beet slices.
3. Sprinkle with toasted walnuts and crumbled goat cheese.
4. Drizzle with olive oil.
5. Toss gently and serve.

Nutritional Values: Cal: 220, Protein: 6g, Carbs: 15g, Fat: 16g, Sodium: 170mg, Fiber: 4g

Tuna and White Bean Salad

PREP: 10 mins
Cook T.: 0 mins
Serves: 2
Ingr:

- 1 can tuna, drained
- 1/2 C white beans, cooked and drained
- 1/4 C red onion, finely chpd
- 2 tbsp olive oil
- 1 tbsp lemon juice

Proc:

1. In a bowl, mix tuna, white beans, and red onion.
2. In a separate small bowl, whisk together olive oil and lemon juice.
3. Pour the dressing over the tuna mixture.
4. Toss gently to combine and serve.

Nutritional Values: Cal: 280, Protein: 25g, Carbs: 20g, Fat: 10g, Sodium: 320mg, Fiber: 5g

Asian-inspired Broccoli and Almond Salad

PREP: 10 mins
Cook T.: 0 mins
Serves: 2
Ingr:

- 2 Cs broccoli florets, blanched
- 1/4 C almonds, toasted and chpd
- 1/4 C red bell pepper, thinly sliced
- 2 tbsp soy sauce (low sodium)
- 1 tbsp sesame oil

Proc:

1. In a large bowl, combine broccoli, almonds, and red bell pepper.
2. In a separate small bowl, whisk together soy sauce and sesame oil.

3. Pour the dressing over the broccoli mixture.
4. Toss to combine and serve.

Nutritional Values: Cal: 190 ,
Protein: 8g, Carbs: 15g, Fat: 12g,
Sodium: 400mg, Fiber: 5g

Grilled Chicken and Mango Salad

PREP: 10 mins
Cook T.: 15 mins
Serves: 2
Ingr:
- 1 chicken breast, grilled and sliced
- 1 mango, peeled and diced
- 2 Cs mixed salad greens
- 2 tbsp olive oil
- 1 tbsp lime juice

Proc:
1. Place salad greens in a large bowl.
2. Top with grilled chicken slices and diced mango.
3. In a small bowl, whisk together olive oil and lime juice.
4. Drizzle the dressing over the salad.
5. Toss gently and serve.

Nutritional Values: Cal: 290,
Protein: 25g, Carbs: 20g, Fat: 12g,
Sodium: 90mg, Fiber: 3g

Roasted Pumpkin and Feta Salad

PREP: 10 mins
Cook T.: 25 mins
Serves: 2
Ingr:
- 1 C pumpkin, roasted and cubed
- 2 Cs spinach leaves
- 1/4 C feta cheese, crumbled
- 2 tbsp pumpkin seeds
- 2 tbsp balsamic vinaigrette

Proc:
1. Place spinach leaves in a large salad bowl.
2. Top with roasted pumpkin cubes.
3. Sprinkle with crumbled feta cheese and pumpkin seeds.
4. Drizzle with balsamic vinaigrette.
5. Toss gently and serve.

Nutritional Values: Cal: 180,
Protein: 6g, Carbs: 15g, Fat: 10g,
Sodium: 250mg, Fiber: 3g

Sweet Potato and Black Bean Salad

PREP: 10 mins
Cook T.: 20 mins
Serves: 2
Ingr:
- 1 sweet potato, roasted and cubed
- 1/2 C black beans, cooked and drained
- 1/4 C red onion, finely chpd
- 2 tbsp olive oil
- 1 tbsp lime juice

Proc:
1. In a large bowl, mix roasted sweet potato cubes, black beans, and red onion.
2. In a separate small bowl, whisk together olive oil and lime juice.
3. Pour the dressing over the sweet potato mixture.
4. Toss gently to combine and serve.

Nutritional Values: Cal: 280,
Protein: 8g, Carbs: 40g, Fat: 10g,
Sodium: 10mg, Fiber: 8g

Cabbage and Apple Slaw

PREP: 10 mins
Cook T.: 0 mins
Serves: 2
Ingr:
- 2 Cs cabbage, shredded
- 1 apple, thinly sliced
- 1/4 C walnuts, chpd
- 2 tbsp olive oil
- 1 tbsp apple cider vinegar

Proc:

1. In a large bowl, combine shredded cabbage, apple slices, and chpd walnuts.
2. In a separate small bowl, whisk together olive oil and apple cider vinegar.
3. Pour the dressing over the cabbage mixture.
4. Toss gently to combine and serve.

Nutritional Values: Cal: 220,
Protein: 4g, Carbs: 20g, Fat: 15g,
Sodium: 20mg, Fiber: 5g

Pear and Blue Cheese Salad

PREP: 10 mins
Cook T.: 0 mins
Serves: 2
Ingr:
- 2 pears, thinly sliced
- 2 Cs mixed salad greens
- 1/4 C blue cheese, crumbled
- 2 tbsp walnuts, toasted and chpd
- 2 tbsp honey

Proc:
1. Place salad greens in a large bowl.
2. Top with pear slices.
3. Sprinkle with crumbled blue cheese and toasted walnuts.
4. Drizzle with honey.
5. Toss gently and serve.

Nutritional Values: Cal: 250,
Protein: 6g, Carbs: 35g, Fat: 10g,
Sodium: 250mg, Fiber: 5g

Wraps and Sandwiches

Grilled Chicken and Avocado Wrap

PREP: 10 mins
Cook T.: 15 mins
Serves: 2
Ingr:
- 1 chicken breast, grilled and sliced
- 1 avocado, sliced
- 2 whole wheat tortillas
- 1/4 C lettuce, shredded
- 2 tbsp Greek yogurt

Proc:
1. Lay out the whole wheat tortillas on a flat surface.
2. Spread a tbsp of Greek yogurt on each tortilla.
3. Place half of the grilled chicken slices and avocado slices on each tortilla.
4. Sprinkle with shredded lettuce.
5. Roll up the tortillas tightly, slice in half, and serve.

Nutritional Values: Cal: 320, Protein: 28g, Carbs: 25g, Fat: 12g, Sodium: 180mg, Fiber: 6g

Tuna and Cucumber Sandwich

PREP: 10 mins
Cook T.: 0 mins
Serves: 2
Ingr:
- 1 can tuna, drained
- 1/4 cucumber, thinly sliced
- 4 slices whole grain bread
- 2 tbsp mayonnaise (low-fat)
- 1 tbsp lemon juice

Proc:
1. In a bowl, mix the drained tuna with mayonnaise and lemon juice.
2. Spread the tuna mixture on two slices of bread.
3. Place cucumber slices on top.
4. Top with the remaining bread slices and press down gently.
5. Slice in half and serve.

Nutritional Values: Cal: 260, Protein: 20g, Carbs: 30g, Fat: 8g, Sodium: 220mg, Fiber: 5g

Turkey and Cranberry Wrap

PREP: 10 mins
Cook T.: 0 mins
Serves: 2
Ingr:
- 4 slices turkey breast
- 2 tbsp cranberry sauce (low-sugar)
- 2 spinach tortillas
- 1/4 C spinach leaves
- 1/4 C feta cheese, crumbled

Proc:
1. Lay out the spinach tortillas on a flat surface.
2. Spread a tbsp of cranberry sauce on each tortilla.

3. Place two slices of turkey breast on each tortilla.
4. Sprinkle with feta cheese and add spinach leaves.
5. Roll up the tortillas tightly, slice in half, and serve.

Nutritional Values: Cal: 280, Protein: 18g, Carbs: 30g, Fat: 10g, Sodium: 250mg, Fiber: 4g

Roasted Vegetable and Hummus Sandwich

PREP: 15 mins
Cook T.: 20 mins
Serves: 2
Ingr:
- 1/2 C mixed vegetables (bell peppers, zucchini), roasted
- 2 tbsp hummus
- 4 slices whole grain bread
- 1/4 C arugula
- 1 tbsp olive oil

Proc:
1. Brush the mixed vegetables with olive oil and roast until tender.
2. Spread a tbsp of hummus on two slices of bread.
3. Place the roasted vegetables on top.
4. Add arugula and top with the remaining bread slices.
5. Press down gently, slice in half, and serve.

Nutritional Values: Cal: 240, Protein: 8g, Carbs: 35g, Fat: 8g, Sodium: 200mg, Fiber: 6g

Egg Salad and Spinach Wrap

PREP: 10 mins
Cook T.: 10 mins
Serves: 2
Ingr:
- 2 eggs, boiled and chpd
- 2 tbsp Greek yogurt
- 2 whole wheat tortillas
- 1/4 C spinach leaves
- 1 tbsp mustard

Proc:
1. In a bowl, mix the chpd eggs with Greek yogurt and mustard.
2. Lay out the tortillas and spread the egg mixture on each.
3. Add spinach leaves.
4. Roll up the tortillas tightly, slice in half, and serve.

Nutritional Values: Cal: 220, Protein: 12g, Carbs: 25g, Fat: 8g, Sodium: 220mg, Fiber: 4g

Grilled Portobello and Pesto Sandwich

PREP: 10 mins
Cook T.: 15 mins
Serves: 2
Ingr:
- 2 Portobello mushrooms, grilled
- 2 tbsp pesto sauce (low-sodium)
- 4 slices whole grain bread
- 1/4 C mozzarella cheese, sliced
- 1 tbsp olive oil

Proc:
1. Brush the Portobello mushrooms with olive oil and grill until tender.

2. Spread a tbsp of pesto sauce on two slices of bread.
3. Place a grilled Portobello mushroom on each.
4. Add mozzarella cheese slices.

5. Top with the remaining bread slices, press down gently, and serve.

Nutritional Values: Cal: 290, Protein: 12g, Carbs: 30g, Fat: 14g, Sodium: 280mg, Fiber: 5g

Chicken Caesar Salad Wrap

PREP: 10 mins
Cook T.: 15 mins
Serves: 2
Ingr:
- 1 chicken breast, grilled and sliced
- 2 tbsp Caesar dressing (low-fat)
- 2 whole wheat tortillas
- 1/4 C romaine lettuce, shredded
- 2 tbsp Parmesan cheese, grated

Proc:
1. Lay out the tortillas and spread a tbsp of Caesar dressing on each.
2. Place half of the grilled chicken slices on each tortilla.
3. Sprinkle with shredded lettuce and grated Parmesan cheese.
4. Roll up the tortillas tightly, slice in half, and serve.

Nutritional Values: Cal: 320, Protein: 28g, Carbs: 25g, Fat: 12g, Sodium: 320mg, Fiber: 3g

Mediterranean Veggie Wrap

PREP: 10 mins
Cook T.: 0 mins
Serves: 2
Ingr:
- 2 whole wheat tortillas
- 1/4 C hummus
- 1/4 C cherry tomatoes, halved
- 1/4 C cucumber, sliced
- 1/4 C feta cheese, crumbled

Proc:
1. Spread an even layer of hummus on each tortilla.

2. Scatter cherry tomatoes and cucumber slices over the hummus.
3. Sprinkle with crumbled feta cheese.
4. Roll up the tortillas tightly, slice in half, and serve.

Nutritional Values: Cal: 240, Protein: 9g, Carbs: 32g, Fat: 9g, Sodium: 290mg, Fiber: 5g

Spicy Tofu Sandwich

PREP: 15 mins
Cook T.: 10 mins
Serves: 2
Ingr:
- 4 slices whole grain bread
- 1/2 C tofu, sliced and pan-fried
- 2 tbsp sriracha mayo

- 1/4 C lettuce, shredded
- 1/4 C carrot, julienned

Proc:
1. Spread sriracha mayo on two slices of bread.
2. Place pan-fried tofu slices on top.

3. Add shredded lettuce and julienned carrot.
4. Top with the remaining bread slices and press down gently.

Nutritional Values: Cal: 260, Protein: 14g, Carbs: 35g, Fat: 8g, Sodium: 310mg, Fiber: 6g

Smoked Salmon and Cream Cheese Wrap

PREP: 10 mins
Cook T.: 0 mins
Serves: 2
Ingr:
- 2 spinach tortillas
- 1/4 C cream cheese (low-fat)
- 1/4 C smoked salmon, sliced
- 1/4 C red onion, thinly sliced
- 1 tbsp capers

Proc:
1. Spread an even layer of cream cheese on each tortilla.
2. Lay out smoked salmon slices over the cream cheese.
3. Add thinly sliced red onion and sprinkle with capers.
4. Roll up the tortillas tightly, slice in half, and serve.

Nutritional Values: Cal: 280, Protein: 18g, Carbs: 30g, Fat: 10g, Sodium: 320mg, Fiber: 4g

Roast Beef and Horseradish Sandwich

PREP: 10 mins
Cook T.: 0 mins
Serves: 2
Ingr:
- 4 slices rye bread
- 1/4 C roast beef, thinly sliced
- 2 tbsp horseradish sauce
- 1/4 C arugula
- 1/4 C Swiss cheese, sliced

Proc:
1. Spread horseradish sauce on two slices of rye bread.
2. Layer roast beef slices and Swiss cheese on top.
3. Add arugula.
4. Top with the remaining bread slices and press down gently.

Nutritional Values: Cal: 290, Protein: 20g, Carbs: 30g, Fat: 10g, Sodium: 330mg, Fiber: 5g

Veggie and Pesto Wrap

PREP: 10 mins
Cook T.: 0 mins
Serves: 2
Ingr:
- 2 tomato tortillas
- 2 tbsp pesto sauce
- 1/4 C bell peppers, thinly sliced
- 1/4 C zucchini, thinly sliced
- 1/4 C mozzarella cheese, shredded

Proc:
1. Spread an even layer of pesto sauce on each tortilla.
2. Scatter bell peppers and zucchini slices over the pesto.
3. Sprinkle with shredded mozzarella cheese.
4. Roll up the tortillas tightly, slice in half, and serve.

Nutritional Values: Cal: 270, Protein: 12g, Carbs: 32g, Fat: 10g, Sodium: 290mg, Fiber: 4g

Soups

Tomato Basil Soup

PREP: 10 mins
Cook T.: 30 mins
Serves: 4
Ingr:
- 4 Cs fresh tomatoes, chpd
- 2 Cs vegetable broth
- 1/4 C fresh basil, chpd
- 1/4 C onions, chpd
- 2 garlic cloves, minced

Proc:
1. In a pot, sauté onions and garlic until translucent.
2. Add tomatoes and vegetable broth, bringing to a boil.
3. Reduce heat and simmer for 20 mins.
4. Blend until smooth, then stir in chpd basil.
5. Serve hot with a sprinkle of fresh basil on top.

Nutritional Values: Cal: 60, Protein: 2g, Carbs: 14g, Fat: 0.5g, Sodium: 150mg, Fiber: 3g

Lentil and Spinach Soup

PREP: 15 mins
Cook T.: 40 mins
Serves: 4
Ingr:
- 1 C lentils, rinsed
- 4 Cs vegetable broth
- 1/2 C spinach, chpd
- 1 onion, chpd
- 2 garlic cloves, minced

Proc:
1. In a pot, sauté onions and garlic until soft.
2. Add lentils and vegetable broth, bringing to a boil.
3. Reduce heat and simmer for 30 mins.
4. Stir in spinach and cook for another 5 mins.

5. Serve hot with a sprinkle of black pepper.

Nutritional Values: Cal: 210, Protein: 14g, Carbs: 36g, Fat: 0.5g, Sodium: 150mg, Fiber: 17g

Carrot Ginger Soup

PREP: 10 mins
Cook T.: 30 mins
Serves: 4
Ingr:
- 4 Cs carrots, chpd
- 4 Cs vegetable broth
- 1 tbsp ginger, minced
- 1 onion, chpd
- 1 tbsp olive oil

Proc:
1. In a pot, heat olive oil and sauté onions and ginger.
2. Add carrots and vegetable broth, bringing to a boil.
3. Reduce heat and simmer until carrots are tender.
4. Blend until smooth and return to the pot to heat.
5. Serve hot with a dollop of yogurt.

Nutritional Values: Cal: 90, Protein: 2g, Carbs: 20g, Fat: 2g, Sodium: 150mg, Fiber: 5g

Cucumber Dill Soup

PREP: 10 mins
Cook T.: 0 mins (chilled soup)
Serves: 4
Ingr:
- 4 Cs cucumber, chpd
- 1/4 C fresh dill, chpd
- 2 Cs plain yogurt
- 1 garlic clove, minced
- 1 tbsp lemon juice

Proc:
1. In a blender, combine cucumber, dill, yogurt, garlic, and lemon juice.
2. Blend until smooth.
3. Chill in the refrigerator for at least 2 hrs.
4. Serve cold with a sprinkle of dill on top.

Nutritional Values: Cal: 70, Protein: 4g, Carbs: 10g, Fat: 2g, Sodium: 50mg, Fiber: 1g

White Bean and Kale Soup

PREP: 15 mins
Cook T.: 40 mins
Serves: 4
Ingr:
- 2 Cs white beans, rinsed
- 4 Cs vegetable broth
- 2 Cs kale, chpd
- 1 onion, chpd
- 2 garlic cloves, minced

Proc:
1. In a pot, sauté onions and garlic until soft.
2. Add white beans, kale, and vegetable broth.
3. Bring to a boil, then reduce heat and simmer for 30 mins.
4. Serve hot with a sprinkle of Parmesan cheese.

Nutritional Values: Cal: 240,
Protein: 15g, Carbs: 44g, Fat: 1g,
Sodium: 150mg, Fiber: 11g

Mushroom Barley Soup

PREP: 15 mins
Cook T.: 50 mins
Serves: 4
Ingr:
- 1 C barley, rinsed
- 4 Cs vegetable broth
- 2 Cs mushrooms, sliced
- 1 onion, chpd
- 2 garlic cloves, minced

Proc:
1. In a pot, sauté onions, garlic, and mushrooms until soft.
2. Add barley and vegetable broth.
3. Bring to a boil, then reduce heat and simmer until barley is tender.
4. Serve hot with a sprinkle of fresh parsley.

Nutritional Values: Cal: 210,
Protein: 6g, Carbs: 44g, Fat: 1g,
Sodium: 150mg, Fiber: 10g

Sweet Potato and Coconut Soup

PREP: 15 mins
Cook T.: 40 mins
Serves: 4
Ingr:
- 4 Cs sweet potato, chpd
- 4 Cs vegetable broth
- 1 can (14 oz) coconut milk
- 1 onion, chpd
- 2 garlic cloves, minced

Proc:
1. In a pot, sauté onions and garlic until soft.
2. Add sweet potatoes, vegetable broth, and coconut milk.
3. Bring to a boil, then reduce heat and simmer until sweet potatoes are tender.
4. Blend until smooth and serve hot with a sprinkle of shredded coconut.

Nutritional Values: Cal: 280,
Protein: 4g, Carbs: 40g, Fat: 12g,
Sodium: 150mg, Fiber: 6g

Broccoli Almond Soup

PREP: 10 mins
Cook T.: 30 mins
Serves: 4
Ingr:
- 4 Cs broccoli, chpd
- 4 Cs vegetable broth
- 1/4 C almonds, toasted
- 1 onion, chpd
- 2 garlic cloves, minced

Proc:
1. In a pot, sauté onions and garlic until soft.
2. Add broccoli and vegetable broth.
3. Bring to a boil, then reduce heat and simmer until broccoli is tender.
4. Blend with toasted almonds until smooth and serve hot.

Nutritional Values: Cal: 110,
Protein: 5g, Carbs: 16g, Fat: 4g,
Sodium: 150mg, Fiber: 5g

Red Pepper and Lentil Soup

PREP: 15 mins
Cook T.: 40 mins
Serves: 4
Ingr:
- 2 Cs red bell peppers, chpd
- 1 C lentils, rinsed
- 4 Cs vegetable broth
- 1 onion, chpd
- 2 garlic cloves, minced

Proc:
1. In a pot, sauté onions and garlic until soft.
2. Add red bell peppers, lentils, and vegetable broth.
3. Bring to a boil, then reduce heat and simmer until lentils are tender.
4. Blend until smooth and serve hot with a sprinkle of black pepper.

Nutritional Values: Cal: 220,
Protein: 14g, Carbs: 40g, Fat: 1g,
Sodium: 150mg, Fiber: 18g

Zucchini and Basil Soup

PREP: 10 mins
Cook T.: 30 mins
Serves: 4
Ingr:
- 4 Cs zucchini, chpd
- 4 Cs vegetable broth
- 1/4 C fresh basil, chpd
- 1 onion, chpd
- 2 garlic cloves, minced

Proc:
1. In a pot, sauté onions and garlic until soft.
2. Add zucchini and vegetable broth.
3. Bring to a boil, then reduce heat and simmer until zucchini is tender.
4. Blend with fresh basil until smooth and serve hot.

Nutritional Values: Cal: 60, Protein:
3g, Carbs: 14g, Fat: 0.5g, Sodium:
150mg, Fiber: 3g

Asparagus and Lemon Soup

PREP: 10 mins
Cook T.: 30 mins
Serves: 4
Ingr:
- 4 Cs asparagus, chpd
- 4 Cs vegetable broth
- 1 tbsp lemon zest
- 1 onion, chpd
- 2 garlic cloves, minced

Proc:
1. In a pot, sauté onions and garlic until soft.
2. Add asparagus and vegetable broth.
3. Bring to a boil, then reduce heat and simmer until asparagus is tender.

4. Blend until smooth, stir in lemon zest, and serve hot.

Nutritional Values: Cal: 70, Protein: 4g, Carbs: 14g, Fat: 0.5g, Sodium: 150mg, Fiber: 4g

Chickpea and Spinach Soup

PREP: 15 mins
Cook T.: 40 mins
Serves: 4
Ingr:

- 2 Cs chickpeas, rinsed and drained
- 4 Cs vegetable broth
- 2 Cs fresh spinach, chpd
- 1 onion, chpd
- 2 garlic cloves, minced

Proc:

1. In a pot, sauté onions and garlic until translucent.
2. Add chickpeas and vegetable broth, bringing the mixture to a boil.
3. Reduce heat and let it simmer for 30 mins.
4. Stir in the chpd spinach and let it cook for another 5-7 mins until wilted.
5. Serve hot with a sprinkle of freshly ground black pepper on top.

Nutritional Values: Cal: 230, Protein: 12g, Carbs: 38g, Fat: 3g, Sodium: 150mg, Fiber: 10g

Chapter 5: Recipes for Dinner

Lean Proteins

Grilled Lemon Herb Chicken

PREP: 10 mins
Cook T.: 15 mins
Serves: 4
Ingr:
- 4 boneless, skinless chicken breasts
- 2 tbsp olive oil
- 1 lemon, zested and juiced
- 2 garlic cloves, minced
- 1 tbsp fresh rosemary, chpd

Proc:
1. In a bowl, mix olive oil, lemon zest, lemon juice, garlic, and rosemary to create a marinade.
2. Marinate the chicken breasts in the mixture for at least 30 mins.
3. Preheat the grill to medium-high heat.
4. Grill the chicken breasts for 6-7 mins on each side or until fully cooked.
5. Serve hot with a slice of lemon and a sprinkle of fresh rosemary.

Nutritional Values: Cal: 210, Protein: 28g, Carbs: 3g, Fat: 9g, Sodium: 70mg, Fiber: 0.5g

Baked Salmon with Dill and Lemon

PREP: 10 mins
Cook T.: 20 mins
Serves: 4
Ingr:
- 4 salmon fillets
- 2 tbsp olive oil
- 1 lemon, sliccd
- 2 tsp fresh dill, chpd
- S/P to taste

Proc:
1. Preheat the oven to 375°F (190°C).
2. Place salmon fillets on a baking sheet and drizzle with olive oil.
3. Season with salt, pepper, and sprinkle with dill.
4. Place lemon slices on top of each fillet.
5. Bake for 20 mins or until salmon easily flakes with a fork.

Nutritional Values: Cal: 230, Protein: 25g, Carbs: 1g, Fat: 14g, Sodium: 60mg, Fiber: 0g

Herb-Crusted Tilapia

PREP: 10 mins
Cook T.: 15 mins
Serves: 4

Ingr:
- 4 tilapia fillets
- 2 tbsp olive oil
- 1 tbsp fresh parsley, chpd

- 1 tsp dried oregano
- S/P to taste

Proc:
1. Preheat the oven to 400°F (200°C).
2. Place tilapia fillets on a baking sheet and brush with olive oil.
3. Season with salt, pepper, parsley, and oregano.
4. Bake for 15 mins or until fish is opaque and flaky.

Nutritional Values: Cal: 180, Protein: 23g, Carbs: 0g, Fat: 9g, Sodium: 50mg, Fiber: 0g

Spiced Turkey Patties

PREP: 15 mins
Cook T.: 10 mins
Serves: 4
Ingr:
- 1 lb ground turkey
- 1 tsp cumin
- 1 tsp paprika
- 2 green onions, finely chpd
- S/P to taste

Proc:
1. In a bowl, mix ground turkey, cumin, paprika, green onions, salt, and pepper.
2. Form into 4 patties.
3. Heat a skillet over medium heat and cook patties for 5 mins on each side or until fully cooked.
4. Serve with a side of mixed greens or your favorite DASH-friendly sauce.

Nutritional Values: Cal: 170, Protein: 22g, Carbs: 1g, Fat: 8g, Sodium: 60mg, Fiber: 0.5g

Lemon Pepper Shrimp Skewers

PREP: 15 mins (plus marinating time)
Cook T.: 10 mins
Serves: 4
Ingr:
- 1 lb large shrimp, peeled and deveined
- 2 tbsp olive oil
- 1 lemon, zested and juiced
- 1 tsp black pepper
- Salt to taste

Proc:
1. In a bowl, mix olive oil, lemon zest, lemon juice, black pepper, and salt to create a marinade.
2. Marinate the shrimp in the mixture for at least 1 hour.
3. Preheat the grill to medium-high heat.
4. Thread the shrimp onto skewers and grill for 2-3 mins on each side or until pink and opaque.
5. Serve immediately with a side of grilled vegetables.

Nutritional Values: Cal: 190, Protein: 24g, Carbs: 2g, Fat: 9g, Sodium: 170mg, Fiber: 0g

Rosemary Lamb Chops

PREP: 10 mins
Cook T.: 15 mins
Serves: 4

Ingr:
- 8 lamb chops
- 2 tbsp olive oil

- 2 tsp fresh rosemary, chpd
- 2 garlic cloves, minced
- S/P to taste

Proc:
1. In a bowl, mix olive oil, rosemary, garlic, salt, and pepper to create a marinade.
2. Marinate the lamb chops in the mixture for at least 30 mins.
3. Preheat the grill to medium-high heat.
4. Grill the lamb chops for 6-7 mins on each side or until your desired level of doneness.
5. Serve hot with a sprinkle of fresh rosemary.

Nutritional Values: Cal: 250, Protein: 21g, Carbs: 1g, Fat: 18g, Sodium: 70mg, Fiber: 0.5g

Tofu Steak with Ginger Soy Glaze

PREP: 10 mins
Cook T.: 15 mins
Serves: 4
Ingr:
- 1 lb firm tofu, sliced into 1-inch steaks
- 2 tbsp soy sauce (low sodium)
- 1 tbsp fresh ginger, grated
- 1 tbsp olive oil
- 1 tsp honey

Proc:
1. In a bowl, mix soy sauce, ginger, olive oil, and honey to create a glaze.
2. Brush the tofu steaks with the glaze.
3. Heat a skillet over medium heat and cook tofu steaks for 5-6 mins on each side or until golden brown.
4. Serve hot with a side of steamed broccoli or green beans.

Nutritional Values: Cal: 150, Protein: 12g, Carbs: 8g, Fat: 8g, Sodium: 250mg, Fiber: 1g

Grilled Portobello Mushrooms

PREP: 10 mins
Cook T.: 15 mins
Serves: 4
Ingr:
- 4 large portobello mushrooms, stems removed
- 2 tbsp olive oil
- 1 tsp balsamic vinegar
- 1 garlic clove, minced
- S/P to taste

Proc:
1. In a bowl, mix olive oil, balsamic vinegar, garlic, salt, and pepper.
2. Brush the mixture onto both sides of the portobello mushrooms.
3. Preheat the grill to medium heat.
4. Grill the mushrooms for 5-6 mins on each side or until tender.
5. Serve hot with a sprinkle of fresh parsley.

Nutritional Values: Cal: 90, Protein: 2g, Carbs: 6g, Fat: 7g, Sodium: 10mg, Fiber: 2g

Balsamic Glazed Chicken Thighs

PREP: 10 mins
Cook T.: 25 mins
Serves: 4
Ingr:

- 8 chicken thighs, skinless and boneless
- 2 tbsp balsamic vinegar
- 1 tbsp olive oil
- 1 tsp honey
- S/P to taste

Proc:

1. In a bowl, mix balsamic vinegar, olive oil, honey, salt, and pepper to create a glaze.
2. Brush the chicken thighs with the glaze.
3. Preheat the oven to 375°F (190°C).
4. Place the chicken thighs on a baking sheet and bake for 25 mins or until fully cooked.
5. Serve hot with a side of roasted vegetables.

Nutritional Values: Cal: 210, Protein: 28g, Carbs: 5g, Fat: 9g, Sodium: 80mg, Fiber: 0g

Spicy Grilled Tempeh

PREP: 10 mins
Cook T.: 15 mins
Serves: 4
Ingr:

- 1 lb tempeh, sliced into 1-inch pieces
- 2 tbsp soy sauce (low sodium)
- 1 tsp chili flakes
- 1 tbsp olive oil
- 1 tsp honey

Proc:

1. In a bowl, mix soy sauce, chili flakes, olive oil, and honey to create a marinade.
2. Marinate the tempeh slices in the mixture for at least 30 mins.
3. Preheat the grill to medium-high heat.
4. Grill the tempeh slices for 5-6 mins on each side or until golden brown.
5. Serve hot with a side of mixed greens.

Nutritional Values: Cal: 220, Protein: 20g, Carbs: 12g, Fat: 12g, Sodium: 250mg, Fiber: 0.5g

Seared Cod with Lemon-Parsley Drizzle

PREP: 10 mins
Cook T.: 12 mins
Serves: 4
Ingr:

- 4 cod fillets
- 2 tbsp olive oil
- 1 lemon, zested and juiced
- 2 tbsp fresh parsley, finely chpd
- S/P to taste

Proc:

1. Season the cod fillets with S/P.
2. In a skillet, heat olive oil over medium-high heat. Once hot, add the cod fillets.
3. Cook for 5-6 mins on each side or until the fish is opaque and flakes easily with a fork.
4. In a small bowl, mix lemon zest, lemon juice, and parsley to create a drizzle.

5. Serve the cod hot, drizzled with the lemon-parsley mixture.

Nutritional Values: Cal: 180, Protein: 23g, Carbs: 1g, Fat: 9g, Sodium: 60mg, Fiber: 0g

Spiced Beef Kebabs

PREP: 15 mins (plus marinating time)
Cook T.: 10 mins
Serves: 4
Ingr:
- 1 lb beef cubes (preferably lean cuts like sirloin or tenderloin)
- 2 tbsp olive oil
- 1 tsp cumin
- 1 tsp paprika
- S/P to taste

Proc:
1. In a bowl, mix olive oil, cumin, paprika, salt, and pepper to create a marinade.
2. Marinate the beef cubes in the mixture for at least 1 hour.
3. Preheat the grill to medium-high heat.
4. Thread the beef cubes onto skewers.
5. Grill for 4-5 mins on each side or until they reach your desired level of doneness.
6. Serve hot with a side of grilled vegetables or a fresh salad.

Nutritional Values: Cal: 240, Protein: 26g, Carbs: 1g, Fat: 15g, Sodium: 70mg, Fiber: 0g

Stews and Curries

Tomato Lentil Stew

PREP: 15 mins
Cook T.: 40 mins
Serves: 4
Ingr:

- 1 C green lentils, rinsed
- 4 Cs vegetable broth
- 2 tomatoes, diced
- 1 onion, chpd
- 2 garlic cloves, minced

Proc:

1. In a pot, sauté onions and garlic until translucent.
2. Add lentils, tomatoes, and vegetable broth.
3. Bring to a boil, then simmer for 35 mins or until lentils are tender.
4. Season with S/P, serve hot.

Nutritional Values: Cal: 220, Protein: 15g, Carbs: 40g, Fat: 1g, Sodium: 300mg, Fiber: 15g

Creamy Coconut Chickpea Curry

PREP: 10 mins
Cook T.: 30 mins
Serves: 4
Ingr:

- 1 can chickpeas, drained
- 1 can coconut milk
- 1 onion, chpd
- 2 tsp curry powder
- 1 tbsp olive oil

Proc:

1. In a pot, heat olive oil and sauté onions until translucent.
2. Add curry powder, chickpeas, and coconut milk.
3. Simmer for 25 mins.
4. Season with S/P, serve hot.

Nutritional Values: Cal: 350, Protein: 10g, Carbs: 30g, Fat: 24g, Sodium: 400mg, Fiber: 8g

Vegetable Quinoa Stew

PREP: 15 mins
Cook T.: 25 mins
Serves: 4
Ingr:

- 1 C quinoa, rinsed
- 4 Cs vegetable broth
- 1 zucchini, chpd
- 1 bell pepper, chpd
- 1 onion, chpd

Proc:

1. In a pot, sauté onion, zucchini, and bell pepper until softened.
2. Add quinoa and vegetable broth.
3. Bring to a boil, then simmer for 20 mins or until quinoa is cooked.
4. Season with S/P, serve hot.

Nutritional Values: Cal: 210, Protein: 8g, Carbs: 40g, Fat: 3g, Sodium: 300mg, Fiber: 5g

Spicy Tofu Curry

PREP: 10 mins
Cook T.: 20 mins
Serves: 4
Ingr:
- 1 block tofu, cubed
- 1 can coconut milk
- 2 tsp red curry paste
- 1 tbsp olive oil
- 1 bell pepper, sliced

Proc:
1. In a pot, heat olive oil and sauté bell pepper for 3 mins.
2. Add tofu cubes and brown slightly.
3. Stir in curry paste and coconut milk, simmer for 15 mins.
4. Season with salt, serve hot.

Nutritional Values: Cal: 300, Protein: 12g, Carbs: 8g, Fat: 26g, Sodium: 200mg, Fiber: 2g

Mushroom and Barley Stew

PREP: 10 mins
Cook T.: 50 mins
Serves: 4
Ingr:
- 1 C barley
- 4 Cs vegetable broth
- 2 Cs mushrooms, sliced
- 1 onion, chpd
- 2 garlic cloves, minced

Proc:
1. In a pot, sauté onions and garlic until translucent.
2. Add mushrooms and cook for 5 mins.
3. Stir in barley and vegetable broth.
4. Bring to a boil, then simmer for 45 mins or until barley is tender.
5. Season with S/P, serve hot.

Nutritional Values: Cal: 220, Protein: 6g, Carbs: 48g, Fat: 1g, Sodium: 300mg, Fiber: 10g

Sweet Potato and Lentil Curry

PREP: 15 mins
Cook T.: 40 mins
Serves: 4
Ingr:
- 2 sweet potatoes, cubed
- 1 C red lentils, rinsed
- 1 can coconut milk
- 2 tsp curry powder
- 1 onion, chpd

Proc:
1. In a pot, sauté onions until translucent.
2. Add sweet potatoes, lentils, curry powder, and coconut milk.
3. Bring to a boil, then simmer for 35 mins or until lentils and sweet potatoes are tender.
4. Season with salt, serve hot.

Nutritional Values: Cal: 380, Protein: 15g, Carbs: 60g, Fat: 10g, Sodium: 100mg, Fiber: 15g

Chicken and Vegetable Stew

PREP: 15 mins
Cook T.: 40 mins
Serves: 4
Ingr:
- 4 chicken breasts, cubed
- 4 Cs chicken broth (low sodium)
- 2 carrots, sliced
- 2 celery stalks, chpd
- 1 onion, chpd

Proc:
1. In a pot, sauté onions, carrots, and celery until softened.
2. Add chicken cubes and brown slightly.
3. Pour in chicken broth and bring to a boil.
4. Simmer for 30 mins or until chicken is cooked through.
5. Season with S/P, serve hot.

Nutritional Values: Cal: 220, Protein: 28g, Carbs: 10g, Fat: 6g, Sodium: 250mg, Fiber: 2g

Beef and Tomato Stew

PREP: 15 mins
Cook T.: 1 hour 30 mins
Serves: 4
Ingr:
- 1 lb beef cubes
- 4 Cs beef broth (low sodium)
- 2 tomatoes, diced
- 1 onion, chpd
- 2 garlic cloves, minced

Proc:
1. In a pot, brown beef cubes on all sides.
2. Add onions and garlic, sauté until translucent.
3. Stir in tomatoes and beef broth.
4. Bring to a boil, then simmer for 1 hour 20 mins or until beef is tender.
5. Season with S/P, serve hot.

Nutritional Values: Cal: 320, Protein: 30g, Carbs: 8g, Fat: 18g, Sodium: 300mg, Fiber: 2g

Fish and Spinach Curry

PREP: 10 mins
Cook T.: 20 mins
Serves: 4
Ingr:
- 4 white fish fillets
- 1 can coconut milk
- 2 Cs fresh spinach
- 2 tsp curry powder
- 1 onion, chpd

Proc:
1. In a pot, sauté onions until translucent.
2. Add fish fillets and brown slightly on both sides.
3. Stir in curry powder, spinach, and coconut milk.
4. Simmer for 15 mins or until fish is cooked through.
5. Season with salt, serve hot.

Nutritional Values: Cal: 280, Protein: 25g, Carbs: 8g, Fat: 18g, Sodium: 150mg, Fiber: 2g

Pumpkin and Bean Stew

PREP: 15 mins
Cook T.: 30 mins
Serves: 4
Ingr:

- 2 Cs pumpkin, cubed
- 1 can white beans, drained
- 4 Cs vegetable broth
- 1 onion, chpd
- 2 tsp cumin

Proc:

1. In a pot, sauté onions until translucent.
2. Add pumpkin cubes and cook for 5 mins.
3. Stir in cumin, beans, and vegetable broth.
4. Bring to a boil, then simmer for 25 mins or until pumpkin is tender.
5. Season with S/P, serve hot.

Nutritional Values: Cal: 220, Protein: 10g, Carbs: 40g, Fat: 2g, Sodium: 300mg, Fiber: 10g

Chickpea and Spinach Curry

PREP: 10 mins
Cook T.: 25 mins
Serves: 4
Ingr:

- 1 can chickpeas, drained and rinsed
- 2 Cs fresh spinach, washed
- 1 can diced tomatoes
- 1 onion, finely chpd
- 2 tsp garam masala

Proc:

1. In a pot, sauté onions until they become translucent.
2. Add garam masala and stir for a minute until fragrant.
3. Pour in the diced tomatoes and chickpeas, bringing the mixture to a simmer.
4. Add spinach and let it wilt into the curry.
5. Simmer for 20 mins, season with salt, and serve hot.

Nutritional Values: Cal: 210, Protein: 9g, Carbs: 35g, Fat: 3g, Sodium: 250mg, Fiber: 8g

Lamb and Green Pea Curry

PREP: 15 mins
Cook T.: 45 mins
Serves: 4
Ingr:

- 1 lb lamb cubes
- 1 C green peas, fresh or frozen
- 1 can coconut milk
- 1 onion, chpd
- 2 tsp curry powder

Proc:

1. In a pot, brown the lamb cubes on all sides.
2. Add onions and sauté until they soften.
3. Sprinkle in the curry powder, stirring to coat the lamb.
4. Pour in the coconut milk and bring the mixture to a simmer.
5. Add green peas and continue to simmer for 40 mins or until lamb is tender. Season with salt and serve hot.

Nutritional Values: Cal: 380, Protein: 28g, Carbs: 12g, Fat: 25g, Sodium: 200mg, Fiber: 4g

Pasta and Grains

Whole Wheat Spaghetti with Garlic and Olive Oil

PREP: 10 mins
Cook T.: 15 mins
Serves: 4
Ingr:
- 12 oz whole wheat spaghetti
- 4 garlic cloves, minced
- 1/4 C olive oil
- Red pepper flakes
- Fresh parsley, chpd

Proc:
1. Cook spaghetti according to package instructions.
2. In a pan, sauté garlic in olive oil until golden.
3. Add red pepper flakes to taste.
4. Toss in cooked spaghetti and mix well.
5. Garnish with fresh parsley.

Nutritional Values: Cal: 320, Protein: 10g, Carbs: 55g, Fat: 10g, Sodium: 10mg, Fiber: 6g

Quinoa and Vegetable Stir Fry

PREP: 15 mins
Cook T.: 20 mins
Serves: 4
Ingr:
- 1 C quinoa
- 2 Cs mixed vegetables (bell peppers, broccoli, carrots)
- 2 tbsp soy sauce (low sodium)
- 1 onion, chpd
- 1 garlic clove, minced

Proc:
1. Cook quinoa according to package instructions.
2. In a pan, sauté onion and garlic until translucent.
3. Add mixed vegetables and stir fry until tender.
4. Mix in cooked quinoa and soy sauce.
5. Serve hot.

Nutritional Values: Cal: 210, Protein: 8g, Carbs: 40g, Fat: 3g, Sodium: 150mg, Fiber: 5g

Brown Rice Pilaf with Almonds

PREP: 10 mins
Cook T.: 45 mins
Serves: 4
Ingr:
- 1 C brown rice
- 2 1/2 Cs water
- 1/4 C almonds, sliced
- 1 onion, finely chpd
- 1 bay leaf

Proc:
1. In a pot, sauté onion until translucent.
2. Add brown rice and stir for 2 mins.
3. Pour in water and add bay leaf.
4. Bring to a boil, then simmer until rice is cooked.
5. Stir in almonds before serving.

Nutritional Values: Cal: 230,
Protein: 6g, Carbs: 45g, Fat: 5g,
Sodium: 10mg, Fiber: 3g

Barley Risotto with Mushrooms

PREP: 10 mins
Cook T.: 40 mins
Serves: 4
Ingr:
- 1 C barley
- 2 Cs mushrooms, sliced
- 4 Cs vegetable broth
- 1 onion, chpd
- 1/4 C parmesan cheese (optional)

Proc:
1. In a pot, sauté onion until translucent.
2. Add mushrooms and cook until browned.
3. Stir in barley, then gradually add vegetable broth, stirring constantly.
4. Cook until barley is tender and creamy.
5. Mix in parmesan cheese if desired.

Nutritional Values: Cal: 240,
Protein: 8g, Carbs: 50g, Fat: 3g,
Sodium: 250mg, Fiber: 10g

Buckwheat Groats with Spinach and Feta

PREP: 10 mins
Cook T.: 20 mins
Serves: 4
Ingr:
- 1 C buckwheat groats
- 2 Cs fresh spinach
- 1/4 C feta cheese, crumbled
- 1 garlic clove, minced
- 2 tbsp olive oil

Proc:
1. Cook buckwheat according to package instructions.
2. In a pan, sauté garlic in olive oil.
3. Add spinach and cook until wilted.
4. Mix in cooked buckwheat and feta cheese.
5. Serve warm.

Nutritional Values: Cal: 220,
Protein: 8g, Carbs: 40g, Fat: 7g,
Sodium: 200mg, Fiber: 5g

Millet Salad with Cucumber and Mint

PREP: 15 mins
Cook T.: 20 mins
Serves: 4
Ingr:
- 1 C millet
- 1 cucumber, diced
- 1/4 C fresh mint, chpd
- 1 lemon, juiced
- 2 tbsp olive oil

Proc:
1. Cook millet according to package instructions, then let it cool.
2. In a bowl, combine millet, cucumber, and mint.
3. Drizzle with olive oil and lemon juice.
4. Toss well and serve chilled.

Nutritional Values: Cal: 210,
Protein: 6g, Carbs: 40g, Fat: 5g,
Sodium: 10mg, Fiber: 4g

Farro with Roasted Vegetables

PREP: 15 mins
Cook T.: 30 mins
Serves: 4
Ingr:

- 1 C farro
- 2 Cs mixed vegetables (zucchini, bell peppers, cherry tomatoes)
- 2 tbsp olive oil
- 1 tsp rosemary, chpd
- Salt to taste

Proc:

1. Cook farro according to package instructions.
2. Toss vegetables in olive oil, rosemary, and salt.
3. Roast in a preheated oven at 400°F for 20 mins.
4. Mix roasted vegetables with cooked farro.
5. Serve warm.

Nutritional Values: Cal: 230, Protein: 7g, Carbs: 45g, Fat: 6g, Sodium: 20mg, Fiber: 8g

Couscous with Chickpeas and Raisins

PREP: 10 mins
Cook T.: 15 mins
Serves: 4
Ingr:

- 1 C couscous
- 1 can chickpeas, drained and rinsed
- 1/4 C raisins
- 1 tsp cumin
- 2 Cs water

Proc:

1. Bring water to a boil, then stir in couscous.
2. Remove from heat and let it sit for 5 mins.
3. Fluff couscous with a fork and add chickpeas, raisins, and cumin.
4. Mix well and serve.

Nutritional Values: Cal: 220, Protein: 8g, Carbs: 45g, Fat: 1g, Sodium: 150mg, Fiber: 6g

Polenta with Tomato Sauce and Basil

PREP: 5 mins
Cook T.: 30 mins
Serves: 4
Ingr:

- 1 C polenta
- 2 Cs tomato sauce
- 1/4 C fresh basil, chpd
- 4 Cs water
- 1 garlic clove, minced

Proc:

1. Bring water to a boil and gradually whisk in polenta.
2. Reduce heat and simmer, stirring frequently, until thickened.
3. In a separate pan, sauté garlic, then add tomato sauce and basil.
4. Serve polenta topped with tomato sauce.

Nutritional Values: Cal: 210, Protein: 4g, Carbs: 45g, Fat: 1g, Sodium: 250mg, Fiber: 4g

Bulgur Wheat with Lemon and Parsley

PREP: 10 mins
Cook T.: 15 mins
Serves: 4
Ingr:
- 1 C bulgur wheat
- 1 lemon, juiced and zested
- 1/4 C fresh parsley, chpd
- 2 Cs water
- 1 tbsp olive oil

Proc:
1. Bring water to a boil and add bulgur wheat.
2. Reduce heat and simmer until water is absorbed.
3. Fluff with a fork and add lemon juice, zest, parsley, and olive oil.
4. Mix well and serve.

Nutritional Values: Cal: 210, Protein: 6g, Carbs: 40g, Fat: 4g, Sodium: 10mg, Fiber: 8g

Rye Berries with Roasted Beets and Goat Cheese

PREP: 15 mins
Cook T.: 45 mins
Serves: 4
Ingr:
- 1 C rye berries
- 2 beets, peeled and diced
- 1/4 C goat cheese, crumbled
- 2 tbsp balsamic vinegar
- 2 Cs water

Proc:
1. Cook rye berries in water until tender.
2. Roast beets in a preheated oven at 400°F for 30 mins.
3. Mix rye berries with roasted beets and drizzle with balsamic vinegar.
4. Top with crumbled goat cheese and serve.

Nutritional Values: Cal: 220, Protein: 7g, Carbs: 40g, Fat: 4g, Sodium: 80mg, Fiber: 6g

Amaranth with Grilled Asparagus and Lemon Vinaigrette

PREP: 10 mins
Cook T.: 20 mins
Serves: 4
Ingr:
- 1 C amaranth
- 1 bunch asparagus, trimmed
- 1 lemon, juiced and zested
- 2 tbsp olive oil
- 2 Cs water

Proc:
1. Cook amaranth in water according to package instructions.
2. Grill asparagus until tender and slightly charred.
3. In a small bowl, whisk together lemon juice, zest, and olive oil to make a vinaigrette.
4. Serve amaranth topped with grilled asparagus and drizzle with the lemon vinaigrette.

Nutritional Values: Cal: 210,
Protein: 7g, Carbs: 35g, Fat: 6g,
Sodium: 10mg, Fiber: 5g

Chapter 6: Recipes for Snacks and Side Dishes

Dips and Spreads

Roasted Red Pepper Hummus

PREP: 10 mins
Cook T.: 5 mins
Serves: 4
Ingr:
- 1 C canned chickpeas, drained
- 1 roasted red pepper
- 1 garlic clove
- 2 tbsp tahini
- 1 tbsp olive oil

Proc:
1. In a food processor, combine chickpeas, roasted red pepper, garlic, and tahini.
2. Blend until smooth.
3. While blending, slowly drizzle in the olive oil.
4. Transfer to a bowl and serve chilled.
5. Garnish with a drizzle of olive oil or a sprinkle of paprika if desired.

Nutritional Values: Cal: 150, Protein: 5g, Carbs: 20g, Fat: 7g, Sodium: 80mg, Fiber: 4g

Avocado And Cilantro Dip

PREP: 10 mins
Cook T.: 0 mins
Serves: 4
Ingr:
- 2 ripe avocados
- 1/4 C fresh cilantro, chpd
- 1 lime, juiced
- 1 small red onion, finely chpd
- Salt to taste

Proc:
1. Halve the avocados and remove the pit.
2. Scoop out the flesh and place it in a bowl.
3. Mash the avocados with a fork.
4. Mix in cilantro, lime juice, and red onion.
5. Season with salt and serve immediately.

Nutritional Values: Cal: 170, Protein: 2g, Carbs: 10g, Fat: 15g, Sodium: 10mg, Fiber: 7g

Sun-Dried Tomato Spread

PREP: 10 mins
Cook T.: 0 mins
Serves: 4
Ingr:
- 1/2 C sun-dried tomatoes, soaked in warm water
- 1/4 C walnuts
- 1 garlic clove

- 1 tbsp olive oil
- Salt to taste

Proc:
1. Drain the sun-dried tomatoes from the water.
2. In a food processor, combine tomatoes, walnuts, and garlic.
3. Blend until a paste forms.
4. While blending, add olive oil in a steady stream.
5. Season with salt and transfer to a bowl.

Nutritional Values: Cal: 120, Protein: 3g, Carbs: 8g, Fat: 10g, Sodium: 50mg, Fiber: 2g

Lemon And Herb Yogurt Dip

PREP: 10 mins
Cook T.: 0 mins
Serves: 4
Ingr:
- 1 C plain Greek yogurt
- 1 lemon, zested and juiced
- 1 tbsp fresh dill, chpd
- 1 tbsp fresh chives, chpd
- Salt to taste

Proc:
1. In a bowl, combine Greek yogurt, lemon zest, and juice.
2. Stir in the fresh herbs.
3. Season with salt and mix well.
4. Chill for at least 30 mins before serving.
5. Garnish with additional herbs if desired.

Nutritional Values: Cal: 60, Protein: 8g, Carbs: 4g, Fat: 1g, Sodium: 40mg, Fiber: 0g

Balsamic Fig And Ricotta Spread

PREP: 10 mins
Cook T.: 5 mins
Serves: 4
Ingr:
- 1/2 C ricotta cheese
- 4 fresh figs, chpd
- 2 tbsp balsamic vinegar
- 1 tbsp honey
- Pinch of salt

Proc:
1. In a saucepan, combine figs, balsamic vinegar, and honey.
2. Cook over medium heat until figs are softened.
3. Let the mixture cool.
4. In a bowl, combine ricotta and the fig mixture.
5. Season with a pinch of salt and serve chilled.

Nutritional Values: Cal: 110, Protein: 4g, Carbs: 15g, Fat: 4g, Sodium: 40mg, Fiber: 1g

Spicy Black Bean Dip

PREP: 10 mins
Cook T.: 0 mins
Serves: 4
Ingr:
- 1 C canned black beans, drained and rinsed
- 1 jalapeño, deseeded and chpd
- 1 garlic clove

- 1 lime, juiced
- Salt to taste

Proc:
1. In a food processor, combine black beans, jalapeño, garlic, and lime juice.
2. Blend until smooth.
3. Season with salt and transfer to a bowl.

4. Serve chilled with a sprinkle of paprika or cayenne pepper for added heat.
5. Garnish with a slice of lime.

Nutritional Values: Cal: 100, Protein: 6g, Carbs: 18g, Fat: 0.5g, Sodium: 10mg, Fiber: 5g

Roasted Garlic And White Bean Dip

PREP: 10 mins
Cook T.: 40 mins
Serves: 4
Ingr:
- 1 head of garlic
- 1 C canned white beans, drained and rinsed
- 2 tbsp olive oil
- 1 lemon, juiced
- Salt to taste

Proc:
1. Preheat oven to 400°F (200°C).
2. Cut the top off the garlic head and drizzle with a tsp of olive oil.

3. Wrap in foil and roast for 35-40 mins until soft.
4. Once cooled, squeeze out the roasted garlic cloves.
5. In a food processor, combine roasted garlic, white beans, olive oil, and lemon juice. Blend until smooth.
6. Season with salt and transfer to a bowl.

Nutritional Values: Cal: 150, Protein: 6g, Carbs: 20g, Fat: 6g, Sodium: 10mg, Fiber: 5g

Tangy Tomato Salsa

PREP: 10 mins
Cook T.: 0 mins
Serves: 4
Ingr:
- 2 ripe tomatoes, chpd
- 1/4 C red onion, finely chpd
- 1 jalapeño, deseeded and minced
- 1 lime, juiced
- Salt to taste

Proc:
1. In a bowl, combine tomatoes, red onion, and jalapeño.
2. Add lime juice and mix well.
3. Season with salt and let it sit for at least 10 mins to meld flavors.
4. Serve chilled with tortilla chips or as a topping for grilled chicken or fish.

Nutritional Values: Cal: 25, Protein: 1g, Carbs: 6g, Fat: 0.2g, Sodium: 5mg, Fiber: 1g

Creamy Cucumber Dill Dip

PREP: 10 mins
Cook T.: 0 mins
Serves: 4
Ingr:

- 1 C plain Greek yogurt
- 1 cucumber, peeled, deseeded, and finely chpd
- 2 tbsp fresh dill, chpd
- 1 garlic clove, minced
- Salt to taste

Proc:

1. In a bowl, combine Greek yogurt, cucumber, dill, and garlic.
2. Mix well until all ingredients are well incorporated.
3. Season with salt and chill for at least 30 mins before serving.
4. Garnish with additional dill or a sprinkle of paprika.

Nutritional Values: Cal: 60, Protein: 8g, Carbs: 5g, Fat: 0.5g, Sodium: 30mg, Fiber: 0g

Sweet Mango Chutney

PREP: 10 mins
Cook T.: 20 mins
Serves: 4
Ingr:

- 2 ripe mangoes, peeled and chpd
- 1/4 C red onion, finely chpd
- 2 tbsp apple cider vinegar
- 1 tbsp honey
- Pinch of salt

Proc:

1. In a saucepan, combine mangoes, red onion, vinegar, and honey.
2. Cook over medium heat until mangoes are soft and the mixture has thickened.
3. Season with a pinch of salt and let it cool.
4. Transfer to a jar and refrigerate. Serve as a spread for toast or as a topping for grilled chicken.

Nutritional Values: Cal: 90, Protein: 1g, Carbs: 22g, Fat: 0.5g, Sodium: 5mg, Fiber: 2g

Zesty Lemon And Herb Tahini

PREP: 10 mins
Cook T.: 0 mins
Serves: 4
Ingr:
- 1/2 C tahini
- 1 lemon, zested and juiced
- 1 garlic clove, minced
- 2 tbsp fresh parsley, chpd
- Water to thin

Proc:
1. In a bowl, combine tahini, lemon zest, juice, garlic, and parsley.
2. Mix well. If the mixture is too thick, add water a tbsp at a time until desired consistency is reached.
3. Season with salt and serve as a dip for vegetables or as a spread for sandwiches.

Nutritional Values: Cal: 170, Protein: 5g, Carbs: 8g, Fat: 15g, Sodium: 10mg, Fiber: 3g

Crunchy Snacks

Roasted Chickpea Crunch

PREP: 10 mins
Cook T.: 40 mins
Serves: 4
Ingr:
- 1 C canned chickpeas, drained and dried
- 1 tbsp olive oil
- 1 tsp smoked paprika
- 1/2 tsp garlic powder
- Salt to taste

Proc:
1. Preheat oven to 375°F (190°C).
2. In a bowl, toss chickpeas with olive oil, smoked paprika, and garlic powder.
3. Spread on a baking sheet in a single layer.
4. Roast for 35-40 mins, stirring occasionally, until crispy.
5. Season with salt and let cool before serving.

Nutritional Values: Cal: 140, Protein: 6g, Carbs: 20g, Fat: 5g, Sodium: 80mg, Fiber: 5g

Baked Kale Chips

PREP: 10 mins
Cook T.: 15 mins
Serves: 4
Ingr:
- 4 Cs kale leaves, washed and dried
- 1 tbsp olive oil
- Salt to taste
- 1/2 tsp garlic powder

Proc:
1. Preheat oven to 350°F (175°C).
2. Toss kale leaves with olive oil in a bowl.
3. Spread on a baking sheet in a single layer.
4. Sprinkle with salt and garlic powder.

5. Bake for 10-15 mins until edges are brown but not burnt.

Nutritional Values: Cal: 60, Protein: 2g, Carbs: 8g, Fat: 3g, Sodium: 80mg, Fiber: 1g

Spicy Roasted Almonds

PREP: 5 mins
Cook T.: 15 mins
Serves: 4
Ingr:
- 1 C raw almonds
- 1 tbsp olive oil
- 1/2 tsp cayenne pepper
- Salt to taste

Proc:
1. Preheat oven to 350°F (175°C).
2. In a bowl, toss almonds with olive oil and cayenne pepper.
3. Spread on a baking sheet in a single layer.
4. Roast for 12-15 mins, stirring occasionally.
5. Season with salt and let cool before serving.

Nutritional Values: Cal: 210, Protein: 8g, Carbs: 8g, Fat: 18g, Sodium: 5mg, Fiber: 4g

Crispy Edamame

PREP: 5 mins
Cook T.: 15 mins
Serves: 4
Ingr:
- 1 C shelled edamame, thawed
- 1 tbsp olive oil
- Salt to taste
- 1/2 tsp garlic powder

Proc:
1. Preheat oven to 400°F (200°C).
2. Toss edamame with olive oil and garlic powder in a bowl.
3. Spread on a baking sheet in a single layer.
4. Roast for 12-15 mins until crispy.
5. Season with salt and serve.

Nutritional Values: Cal: 100, Protein: 9g, Carbs: 7g, Fat: 5g, Sodium: 10mg, Fiber: 3g

Roasted Pumpkin Seeds

PREP: 10 mins
Cook T.: 20 mins
Serves: 4
Ingr:
- 1 C pumpkin seeds, cleaned and dried
- 1 tbsp olive oil
- Salt to taste
- 1/2 tsp smoked paprika

Proc:
1. Preheat oven to 325°F (165°C).
2. Toss pumpkin seeds with olive oil and smoked paprika in a bowl.
3. Spread on a baking sheet in a single layer.
4. Roast for 15-20 mins, stirring occasionally, until golden brown.
5. Season with salt and let cool before serving.

Nutritional Values: Cal: 180, Protein: 9g, Carbs: 4g, Fat: 15g, Sodium: 5mg, Fiber: 2g

Crunchy Beet Chips

PREP: 10 mins
Cook T.: 25 mins
Serves: 4
Ingr:
- 2 medium beets, thinly sliced
- 1 tbsp olive oil
- Salt to taste

Proc:
1. Preheat oven to 375°F (190°C).
2. Toss beet slices with olive oil in a bowl.
3. Spread on a baking sheet in a single layer.
4. Bake for 20-25 mins, turning once, until crispy.
5. Season with salt and let cool before serving.

Nutritional Values: Cal: 60, Protein: 1g, Carbs: 8g, Fat: 3g, Sodium: 80mg, Fiber: 2g

Baked Zucchini Chips

PREP: 10 mins
Cook T.: 25 mins
Serves: 4
Ingr:
- 2 medium zucchinis, thinly sliced
- 1 tbsp olive oil
- Salt to taste
- 1/2 tsp garlic powder

Proc:
1. Preheat oven to 375°F (190°C).
2. Toss zucchini slices with olive oil and garlic powder in a bowl.
3. Spread on a baking sheet in a single layer.
4. Bake for 20-25 mins, turning once, until crispy.
5. Season with salt and let cool before serving.

Nutritional Values: Cal: 50, Protein: 1g, Carbs: 6g, Fat: 3g, Sodium: 10mg, Fiber: 1g

Spicy Roasted Cashews

PREP: 5 mins
Cook T.: 15 mins
Serves: 4
Ingr:
- 1 C raw cashews
- 1 tbsp olive oil
- 1/2 tsp chili powder
- Salt to taste

Proc:
1. Preheat oven to 350°F (175°C).
2. In a bowl, toss cashews with olive oil and chili powder.
3. Spread on a baking sheet in a single layer.
4. Roast for 12-15 mins, stirring occasionally.
5. Season with salt and let cool before serving.

Nutritional Values: Cal: 200, Protein: 5g, Carbs: 12g, Fat: 16g, Sodium: 5mg, Fiber: 1g

Crispy Brussels Sprout Chips

PREP: 10 mins
Cook T.: 20 mins
Serves: 4
Ingr:
- 12 Brussels sprouts, leaves separated
- 1 tbsp olive oil
- Salt to taste
- 1/2 tsp garlic powder

Proc:
1. Preheat oven to 375°F (190°C).
2. Toss Brussels sprout leaves with olive oil and garlic powder in a bowl.
3. Spread on a baking sheet in a single layer.
4. Bake for 15-20 mins, turning once, until crispy.
5. Season with salt and let cool before serving.

Nutritional Values: Cal: 60, Protein: 3g, Carbs: 8g, Fat: 3g, Sodium: 10mg, Fiber: 3g

Roasted Sweet Potato Wedges

PREP: 10 mins
Cook T.: 30 mins
Serves: 4
Ingr:
- 2 medium sweet potatoes, cut into wedges
- 1 tbsp olive oil
- Salt to taste
- 1/2 tsp smoked paprika

Proc:
1. Preheat oven to 400°F (200°C).
2. Toss sweet potato wedges with olive oil and smoked paprika in a bowl.
3. Spread on a baking sheet in a single layer.
4. Bake for 25-30 mins, turning once, until golden brown and crispy.
5. Season with salt and serve.

Nutritional Values: Cal: 110, Protein: 2g, Carbs: 26g, Fat: 3g, Sodium: 70mg, Fiber: 4g

Crunchy Green Pea Snack

PREP: 5 mins
Cook T.: 20 mins
Serves: 4
Ingr:
- 1 C frozen green peas, thawed
- 1 tbsp olive oil
- Salt to taste
- 1/2 tsp onion powder

Proc:
1. Preheat oven to 375°F (190°C).
2. Toss green peas with olive oil and onion powder in a bowl.
3. Spread on a baking sheet in a single layer.
4. Roast for 18-20 mins, stirring occasionally, until crispy.
5. Season with salt and let cool before serving.

Nutritional Values: Cal: 70, Protein: 4g, Carbs: 11g, Fat: 2g, Sodium: 10mg, Fiber: 4g

Crispy Cauliflower Bites

PREP: 10 mins
Cook T.: 25 mins
Serves: 4
Ingr:
- 2 Cs cauliflower florets
- 1 tbsp olive oil
- Salt to taste
- 1/2 tsp turmeric powder

Proc:
1. Preheat oven to 400°F (200°C).
2. Toss cauliflower florets with olive oil and turmeric in a bowl.
3. Spread on a baking sheet in a single layer.
4. Roast for 20-25 mins, turning once, until golden brown and crispy.
5. Season with salt and serve.

Nutritional Values: Cal: 50, Protein: 2g, Carbs: 6g, Fat: 3g, Sodium: 20mg, Fiber: 2g

Vegetable Sides

Roasted Brussels Sprouts With Garlic

PREP: 10 mins
Cook T.: 25 mins
Serves: 4
Ingr:

- 2 Cs Brussels sprouts, halved
- 2 tbsp olive oil
- 3 garlic cloves, minced
- Salt to taste
- Freshly ground black pepper

Proc:

1. Preheat oven to 400°F (200°C).
2. Toss Brussels sprouts with olive oil, garlic, salt, and pepper.
3. Spread on a baking sheet.
4. Roast for 20-25 mins until tender and slightly crispy.
5. Serve warm.

Nutritional Values: Cal: 80, Protein: 3g, Carbs: 10g, Fat: 4g, Sodium: 20mg, Fiber: 4g

Steamed Green Beans With Lemon Zest

PREP: 5 mins
Cook T.: 10 mins
Serves: 4
Ingr:

- 2 Cs fresh green beans, trimmed
- Zest of 1 lemon
- 1 tbsp olive oil
- Salt to taste

Proc:

1. Steam green beans until tender-crisp, about 7-8 mins.
2. Toss with olive oil, lemon zest, and salt.
3. Serve immediately.

Nutritional Values: Cal: 50, Protein: 2g, Carbs: 7g, Fat: 2g, Sodium: 10mg, Fiber: 3g

Sautéed Spinach With Nutmeg

PREP: 5 mins
Cook T.: 5 mins
Serves: 4
Ingr:

- 4 Cs fresh spinach
- 1 tbsp olive oil
- Pinch of nutmeg
- Salt to taste

Proc:

1. Heat olive oil in a pan.
2. Add spinach and sauté until wilted.
3. Season with nutmeg and salt.
4. Serve warm.

Nutritional Values: Cal: 40, Protein: 2g, Carbs: 3g, Fat: 3g, Sodium: 50mg, Fiber: 1g

Grilled Zucchini Slices

PREP: 10 mins
Cook T.: 10 mins
Serves: 4
Ingr:
- 2 medium zucchinis, sliced lengthwise
- 2 tbsp olive oil
- Salt to taste
- Freshly ground black pepper

Proc:
1. Preheat grill to medium-high.
2. Brush zucchini slices with olive oil and season with S/P.
3. Grill for 4-5 mins on each side until tender.
4. Serve immediately.

Nutritional Values: Cal: 70, Protein: 2g, Carbs: 6g, Fat: 5g, Sodium: 10mg, Fiber: 2g

Roasted Beet Salad

PREP: 10 mins
Cook T.: 45 mins
Serves: 4
Ingr:
- 4 medium beets, peeled and diced
- 2 tbsp olive oil
- Salt to taste
- Freshly ground black pepper

Proc:
1. Preheat oven to 375°F (190°C).
2. Toss beets with olive oil, salt, and pepper.
3. Spread on a baking sheet.
4. Roast for 40-45 mins until tender.
5. Serve warm or cold.

Nutritional Values: Cal: 90, Protein: 2g, Carbs: 13g, Fat: 4g, Sodium: 50mg, Fiber: 4g

Simple Cabbage Stir-Fry

PREP: 10 mins
Cook T.: 15 mins
Serves: 4
Ingr:
- 4 Cs shredded cabbage
- 2 tbsp olive oil
- 2 garlic cloves, minced
- Salt to taste

Proc:
1. Heat olive oil in a large pan.
2. Add garlic and sauté for a minute.
3. Add shredded cabbage and stir-fry until tender.
4. Season with salt and serve.

Nutritional Values: Cal: 70, Protein: 2g, Carbs: 8g, Fat: 4g, Sodium: 20mg, Fiber: 3g

Balsamic Roasted Carrots

PREP: 10 mins
Cook T.: 30 mins
Serves: 4
Ingr:
- 4 large carrots, peeled and sliced
- 2 tbsp olive oil
- 2 tbsp balsamic vinegar
- Salt to taste

Proc:

1. Preheat oven to 400°F (200°C).
2. Toss carrots with olive oil, balsamic vinegar, and salt.
3. Spread on a baking sheet.
4. Roast for 25-30 mins until tender.
5. Serve warm.

Nutritional Values: Cal: 80, Protein: 1g, Carbs: 10g, Fat: 4g, Sodium: 50mg, Fiber: 3g

Garlic Broccoli Florets

PREP: 5 mins
Cook T.: 10 mins
Serves: 4
Ingr:
- 4 Cs broccoli florets
- 2 tbsp olive oil
- 3 garlic cloves, minced
- Salt to taste

Proc:

1. Heat olive oil in a pan.
2. Add garlic and sauté for a minute.
3. Add broccoli florets and stir-fry until bright green and slightly tender.
4. Season with salt and serve.

Nutritional Values: Cal: 80, Protein: 3g, Carbs: 8g, Fat: 5g, Sodium: 20mg, Fiber: 3g

Lemon-Herb Asparagus

PREP: 5 mins
Cook T.: 10 mins
Serves: 4
Ingr:
- 2 Cs fresh asparagus, trimmed
- 1 tbsp olive oil
- Zest of 1 lemon
- 1 tsp dried mixed herbs (like basil, oregano)
- Salt to taste

Proc:

1. Heat olive oil in a pan.
2. Add asparagus and sauté until tender-crisp.
3. Season with lemon zest, mixed herbs, and salt.
4. Serve immediately.

Nutritional Values: Cal: 50, Protein: 2g, Carbs: 5g, Fat: 3g, Sodium: 10mg, Fiber: 2g

Simple Sautéed Kale

PREP: 5 mins
Cook T.: 10 mins
Serves: 4
Ingr:
- 4 Cs fresh kale, chpd
- 1 tbsp olive oil
- 2 garlic cloves, minced
- Salt to taste

Proc:
1. Heat olive oil in a large pan.
2. Add garlic and sauté for a minute.
3. Add kale and sauté until wilted and tender.
4. Season with salt and serve.

Nutritional Values: Cal: 60, Protein: 3g, Carbs: 7g, Fat: 3g, Sodium: 30mg, Fiber: 2g

Roasted Red Peppers

PREP: 5 mins
Cook T.: 20 mins
Serves: 4
Ingr:
- 2 large red bell peppers, sliced
- 1 tbsp olive oil
- Salt to taste
- Freshly ground black pepper

Proc:
1. Preheat oven to 400°F (200°C).
2. Toss bell pepper slices with olive oil, salt, and pepper.
3. Spread on a baking sheet.
4. Roast for 15-20 mins until tender and slightly charred.
5. Serve warm.

Nutritional Values: Cal: 50, Protein: 1g, Carbs: 6g, Fat: 3g, Sodium: 10mg, Fiber: 2g

Chapter 7: Recipes for Desserts and Sweets

Fruit-Based Desserts

Berry Medley Parfait

PREP: 10 mins
Cook T.: 0 mins
Serves: 2
Ingr:

- 1 C mixed berries (strawberries, blueberries, raspberries)
- 1 C low-fat yogurt
- 2 tbsp honey
- 1 tsp vanilla extract
- 2 tbsp granola

Proc:

1. In a bowl, mix yogurt, honey, and vanilla extract.
2. In serving glasses, layer a spoonful of the yogurt mixture.
3. Add a layer of mixed berries.
4. Repeat layers until glasses are filled, finishing with berries on top.
5. Sprinkle granola on top and serve.

Nutritional Values: Cal: 180, Protein: 5g, Carbs: 35g, Fat: 2g, Sodium: 40mg, Fiber: 3g

Citrus Fruit Salad

PREP: 15 mins
Cook T.: 0 mins
Serves: 4
Ingr:

- 2 oranges, segmented
- 2 grapefruits, segmented
- 1 tbsp honey
- 1 tsp fresh mint, chpd
- Zest of 1 lemon

Proc:

1. In a large bowl, combine orange and grapefruit segments.
2. Drizzle honey over the fruit.
3. Sprinkle with fresh mint and lemon zest.
4. Toss gently to combine.
5. Chill for 10 mins before serving.

Nutritional Values: Cal: 90, Protein: 1g, Carbs: 22g, Fat: 0.5g, Sodium: 0mg, Fiber: 3g

Baked Apples With Cinnamon

PREP: 10 mins
Cook T.: 30 mins
Serves: 4
Ingr:

- 4 medium apples
- 2 tsp cinnamon
- 2 tbsp honey
- 1/4 C water
- 1 tsp vanilla extract

Proc:

1. Preheat oven to 350°F (175°C).
2. Core the apples and place them in a baking dish.
3. Drizzle honey and sprinkle cinnamon over each apple.
4. Add water and vanilla to the baking dish.
5. Bake for 30 mins or until apples are tender.

Nutritional Values: Cal: 110, Protein: 0.5g, Carbs: 29g, Fat: 0.3g, Sodium: 2mg, Fiber: 4g

Mango Sorbet

PREP: 10 mins (plus freezing time)
Cook T.: 0 mins
Serves: 4
Ingr:

- 2 ripe mangoes, peeled and pitted
- 2 tbsp honey
- 1 tbsp lemon juice
- 1/2 C water

Proc:

1. Blend mangoes, honey, lemon juice, and water until smooth.
2. Pour the mixture into a shallow dish and freeze.
3. Once frozen, break into chunks and blend again until creamy.
4. Freeze again for 2 hrs before serving.

Nutritional Values: Cal: 120, Protein: 1g, Carbs: 31g, Fat: 0.5g, Sodium: 3mg, Fiber: 2g

Banana And Berry Smoothie Bowl

PREP: 10 mins
Cook T.: 0 mins
Serves: 2
Ingr:

- 2 ripe bananas
- 1 C mixed berries
- 1/2 C low-fat yogurt
- 1 tbsp honey
- 1 tsp chia seeds

Proc:

1. Blend bananas, half of the mixed berries, yogurt, and honey until smooth.
2. Pour into bowls.
3. Top with the remaining berries and sprinkle chia seeds.
4. Serve immediately.

Nutritional Values: Cal: 210, Protein: 5g, Carbs: 47g, Fat: 2g, Sodium: 35mg, Fiber: 6g

Grilled Pineapple Slices

PREP: 10 mins
Cook T.: 10 mins
Serves: 4
Ingr:

- 4 pineapple slices
- 1 tbsp honey
- 1 tsp cinnamon
- Zest of 1 lime

Proc:

1. Preheat grill to medium-high.
2. Brush pineapple slices with honey and sprinkle with cinnamon.

3. Grill for 4-5 mins on each side until caramelized.
4. Sprinkle with lime zest and serve.

Nutritional Values: Cal: 60, Protein: 0.5g, Carbs: 16g, Fat: 0.2g, Sodium: 1mg, Fiber: 1g

Strawberry And Kiwi Tart

PREP: 20 mins
Cook T.: 15 mins
Serves: 4
Ingr:
- 1 pre-made whole wheat tart crust
- 1 C strawberries, sliced
- 2 kiwis, peeled and sliced
- 2 tbsp honey
- 1/2 C low-fat yogurt

Proc:
1. Preheat oven to 350°F (175°C).
2. Bake the tart crust for 10-12 mins or until golden.
3. Allow to cool.
4. Spread yogurt over the cooled crust.
5. Arrange strawberries and kiwi slices on top.
6. Drizzle with honey and serve.

Nutritional Values: Cal: 210, Protein: 4g, Carbs: 40g, Fat: 5g, Sodium: 120mg, Fiber: 4g

Peach And Raspberry Crumble

PREP: 15 mins
Cook T.: 25 mins
Serves: 4
Ingr:
- 2 peaches, sliced
- 1 C raspberries
- 2 tbsp honey
- 1/2 C granola
- 1 tsp cinnamon

Proc:
1. Preheat oven to 375°F (190°C).
2. In a baking dish, mix peaches, raspberries, and honey.
3. Sprinkle granola and cinnamon on top.
4. Bake for 20-25 mins until the top is golden and the fruit is bubbly.
5. Serve warm.

Nutritional Values: Cal: 140, Protein: 3g, Carbs: 30g, Fat: 2g, Sodium: 10mg, Fiber: 4g

Melon Ball Salad

PREP: 15 mins
Cook T.: 0 mins
Serves: 4
Ingr:
- 1 C watermelon balls
- 1 C cantaloupe balls
- 1 C honeydew balls
- 1 tbsp fresh mint, chpd
- Zest of 1 lemon

Proc:
1. In a large bowl, combine watermelon, cantaloupe, and honeydew balls.
2. Sprinkle with fresh mint and lemon zest.
3. Toss gently to combine.
4. Chill for 10 mins before serving.

Nutritional Values: Cal: 60, Protein: 1g, Carbs: 15g, Fat: 0.3g, Sodium: 15mg, Fiber: 1g

Blueberry And Lemon Sorbet

PREP: 10 mins (plus freezing time)
Cook T.: 0 mins
Serves: 4
Ingr:
- 2 Cs blueberries
- 2 tbsp honey
- 1 tbsp lemon juice
- Zest of 1 lemon
- 1/2 C water

Proc:
1. Blend blueberries, honey, lemon juice, zest, and water until smooth.
2. Pour the mixture into a shallow dish and freeze.
3. Once frozen, break into chunks and blend again until creamy.
4. Freeze again for 2 hrs before serving.

Nutritional Values: Cal: 90, Protein: 1g, Carbs: 23g, Fat: 0.5g, Sodium: 5mg, Fiber: 3g

Tropical Fruit Popsicles

PREP: 10 mins (plus freezing time)
Cook T.: 0 mins
Serves: 6
Ingr:
- 1 C pineapple chunks
- 1 C mango chunks
- 1/2 C coconut water
- 1 tbsp honey
- 1 tsp lime juice

Proc:
1. Blend pineapple, mango, coconut water, honey, and lime juice until smooth.
2. Pour the mixture into popsicle molds.
3. Freeze for at least 4 hrs or until solid.
4. Remove from molds and serve.

Nutritional Values: Cal: 70, Protein: 1g, Carbs: 18g, Fat: 0.5g, Sodium: 15mg, Fiber: 2g

Cherry And Almond Clusters

PREP: 10 mins (plus chilling time)
Cook T.: 5 mins
Serves: 4
Ingr:
- 1 C fresh cherries, pitted and halved
- 1/4 C almonds, chpd
- 2 tbsp honey
- 1 tsp vanilla extract
- A pinch of sea salt

Proc:
1. In a saucepan, heat honey and vanilla extract over low heat until it becomes slightly more fluid.
2. Add cherries and almonds to the saucepan, stirring to coat them with the honey mixture.
3. Spoon small clusters of the cherry and almond mixture onto a parchment-lined tray.

4. Sprinkle a tiny pinch of sea salt over each cluster.
5. Chill in the refrigerator for at least 2 hrs or until set.

Nutritional Values: Cal: 110, Protein: 2g, Carbs: 18g, Fat: 4g, Sodium: 20mg, Fiber: 2g

Cakes and Muffins

Lemon And Poppy Seed Muffins

PREP: 15 mins
Cook T.: 20 mins
Serves: 6
Ingr:
- 1 C whole wheat flour
- 1/4 C honey
- 1 tsp baking powder
- 1 lemon (zest and juice)
- 1 tbsp poppy seeds

Proc:
1. Preheat oven to 350°F (175°C) and line a muffin tin with paper liners.
2. In a bowl, combine flour, baking powder, lemon zest, and poppy seeds.
3. Stir in honey and lemon juice until just combined.
4. Divide batter among muffin Cs and bake for 20 mins or until a toothpick comes out clean.
5. Allow to cool before serving.

Nutritional Values: Cal: 110, Protein: 3g, Carbs: 24g, Fat: 1g, Sodium: 80mg, Fiber: 3g

Cinnamon Apple Cake

PREP: 15 mins
Cook T.: 30 mins
Serves: 8
Ingr:
- 2 apples, peeled and diced
- 1 C whole wheat flour
- 1/4 C maple syrup
- 1 tsp cinnamon
- 1 tsp baking soda

Proc:
1. Preheat oven to 350°F (175°C) and grease an 8-inch round cake pan.
2. In a bowl, combine flour, cinnamon, and baking soda.
3. Stir in maple syrup and diced apples.
4. Pour batter into the prepared pan and bake for 30 mins or until a toothpick comes out clean.
5. Allow to cool before slicing and serving.

Nutritional Values: Cal: 120, Protein: 3g, Carbs: 27g, Fat: 1g, Sodium: 150mg, Fiber: 4g

Blueberry Oat Muffins

PREP: 10 mins
Cook T.: 25 mins
Serves: 6
Ingr:
- 1 C rolled oats
- 1/2 C almond milk
- 1/4 C honey
- 1 tsp baking powder
- 1/2 C fresh blueberries

Proc:
1. Preheat oven to 350°F (175°C) and line a muffin tin with paper liners.
2. In a bowl, mix oats, baking powder, and blueberries.

3. Add almond milk and honey, stirring until combined.
4. Divide batter among muffin Cs and bake for 25 mins or until golden brown.
5. Allow to cool before serving.

Nutritional Values: Cal: 115, Protein: 3g, Carbs: 25g, Fat: 2g, Sodium: 80mg, Fiber: 3g

Chocolate Zucchini Muffins

PREP: 15 mins
Cook T.: 20 mins
Serves: 6
Ingr:
- 1 zucchini, grated
- 1 C whole wheat flour
- 1/4 C cocoa powder
- 1/4 C maple syrup
- 1 tsp baking soda

Proc:
1. Preheat oven to 350°F (175°C) and line a muffin tin with paper liners.
2. In a bowl, combine flour, cocoa powder, and baking soda.
3. Stir in maple syrup and grated zucchini.
4. Divide batter among muffin Cs and bake for 20 mins or until a toothpick comes out clean.
5. Allow to cool before serving.

Nutritional Values: Cal: 120, Protein: 4g, Carbs: 26g, Fat: 2g, Sodium: 150mg, Fiber: 4g

Carrot And Walnut Cake

PREP: 20 mins
Cook T.: 35 mins
Serves: 8
Ingr:
- 2 carrots, grated
- 1 C whole wheat flour
- 1/4 C chpd walnuts
- 1/4 C honey
- 1 tsp baking powder

Proc:
1. Preheat oven to 350°F (175°C) and grease an 8-inch round cake pan.
2. In a bowl, combine flour, baking powder, and walnuts.
3. Stir in honey and grated carrots.
4. Pour batter into the prepared pan and bake for 35 mins or until a toothpick comes out clean.
5. Allow to cool before slicing and serving.

Nutritional Values: Cal: 130, Protein: 4g, Carbs: 28g, Fat: 3g, Sodium: 100mg, Fiber: 4g

Banana And Coconut Muffins

PREP: 10 mins
Cook T.: 20 mins
Serves: 6
Ingr:
- 2 ripe bananas, mashed
- 1 C whole wheat flour
- 1/4 C shredded coconut
- 1/4 C honey
- 1 tsp baking soda

Proc:
1. Preheat oven to 350°F (175°C) and line a muffin tin with paper

liners.
2. In a bowl, combine flour, baking soda, and shredded coconut.
3. Stir in honey and mashed bananas.

4. Divide batter among muffin Cs and bake for 20 mins or until golden brown.
5. Allow to cool before serving.
Nutritional Values: Cal: 140, Protein: 3g, Carbs: 31g, Fat: 2g, Sodium: 150mg, Fiber: 4g

Vanilla And Berry Cake

PREP: 15 mins
Cook T.: 30 mins
Serves: 8
Ingr:
- 1 C mixed berries (blueberries, raspberries, strawberries)
- 1 C whole wheat flour
- 1/4 C honey
- 1 tsp vanilla extract
- 1 tsp baking powder

Proc:
1. Preheat oven to 350°F (175°C) and grease an 8-inch round cake pan.

2. In a bowl, combine flour, baking powder, and mixed berries.
3. Stir in honey and vanilla extract.
4. Pour batter into the prepared pan and bake for 30 mins or until a toothpick comes out clean.
5. Allow to cool before slicing and serving.
Nutritional Values: Cal: 110, Protein: 3g, Carbs: 25g, Fat: 1g, Sodium: 100mg, Fiber: 3g

Peach And Almond Muffins

PREP: 15 mins
Cook T.: 20 mins
Serves: 6
Ingr:
- 2 peaches, diced
- 1 C whole wheat flour
- 1/4 C chpd almonds
- 1/4 C honey
- 1 tsp baking powder

Proc:
1. Preheat oven to 350°F (175°C) and line a muffin tin with paper liners.

2. In a bowl, combine flour, baking powder, and chpd almonds.
3. Stir in honey and diced peaches.
4. Divide batter among muffin Cs and bake for 20 mins or until a toothpick comes out clean.
5. Allow to cool before serving.
Nutritional Values: Cal: 130, Protein: 4g, Carbs: 28g, Fat: 3g, Sodium: 100mg, Fiber: 3g

Chocolate And Orange Cake

PREP: 20 mins
Cook T.: 35 mins
Serves: 8

Ingr:
- 1 orange (zest and juice)
- 1 C whole wheat flour

- 1/4 C cocoa powder
- 1/4 C honey
- 1 tsp baking soda

Proc:
1. Preheat oven to 350°F (175°C) and grease an 8-inch round cake pan.
2. In a bowl, combine flour, cocoa powder, and baking soda.
3. Stir in honey, orange zest, and orange juice.
4. Pour batter into the prepared pan and bake for 35 mins or until a toothpick comes out clean.
5. Allow to cool before slicing and serving.

Nutritional Values: Cal: 120, Protein: 4g, Carbs: 27g, Fat: 2g, Sodium: 150mg, Fiber: 4g

Strawberry And Cream Muffins

PREP: 10 mins
Cook T.: 20 mins
Serves: 6
Ingr:
- 1/2 C strawberries, diced
- 1 C whole wheat flour
- 1/4 C low-fat cream
- 1/4 C honey
- 1 tsp baking powder

Proc:
1. Preheat oven to 350°F (175°C) and line a muffin tin with paper liners.
2. In a bowl, combine flour and baking powder.
3. Stir in honey, cream, and diced strawberries.
4. Divide batter among muffin Cs and bake for 20 mins or until golden brown.
5. Allow to cool before serving.

Nutritional Values: Cal: 130, Protein: 3g, Carbs: 29g, Fat: 2g, Sodium: 100mg, Fiber: 3g

Raspberry Coconut Muffins

PREP: 10 mins
Cook T.: 20 mins
Serves: 6
Ingr:
- 1/2 C raspberries
- 1 C whole wheat flour
- 1/4 C shredded coconut
- 1/4 C honey
- 1 tsp baking powder

Proc:
1. Preheat oven to 350°F (175°C) and line a muffin tin with paper liners.
2. In a bowl, combine flour, baking powder, and shredded coconut.
3. Stir in honey and gently fold in raspberries.
4. Divide batter among muffin Cs and bake for 20 mins or until a toothpick comes out clean.
5. Allow to cool before serving.

Nutritional Values: Cal: 135, Protein: 3g, Carbs: 30g, Fat: 2g, Sodium: 90mg, Fiber: 4g

Pear And Cinnamon Cake

PREP: 15 mins
Cook T.: 30 mins
Serves: 8
Ingr:

- 2 ripe pears, diced
- 1 C whole wheat flour
- 1/4 C honey
- 1 tsp cinnamon
- 1 tsp baking soda

Proc:

1. Preheat oven to 350°F (175°C) and grease an 8-inch round cake pan.
2. In a bowl, combine flour, cinnamon, and baking soda.
3. Stir in honey and fold in diced pears.
4. Pour batter into the prepared pan and bake for 30 mins or until a toothpick comes out clean.
5. Allow to cool before slicing and serving.

Nutritional Values: Cal: 125, Protein: 3g, Carbs: 28g, Fat: 1g, Sodium: 140mg, Fiber: 4g

Frozen Treats

Mango Banana Sorbet

PREP: 10 mins
Cook T.: 4 hrs (freezing)
Serves: 4
Ingr:
- 2 ripe bananas
- 1 ripe mango
- 1 tsp lemon juice
- 2 tbsp honey
- A pinch of salt

Proc:
1. Blend all ingredients until smooth.
2. Pour into a container and freeze for 4 hrs.
3. Scoop and serve.

Nutritional Values: Cal: 110, Protein: 1g, Carbs: 28g, Fat: 0.5g, Sodium: 10mg, Fiber: 3g

Berry Yogurt Popsicles

PREP: 15 mins
Cook T.: 6 hrs (freezing)
Serves: 6
Ingr:
- 2 Cs mixed berries (strawberries, blueberries, raspberries)
- 1 C low-fat yogurt
- 2 tbsp honey
- 1 tsp vanilla extract
- A pinch of salt

Proc:
1. Blend berries, yogurt, honey, vanilla, and salt until smooth.
2. Pour into popsicle molds and insert sticks.
3. Freeze for 6 hrs or until set.

Nutritional Values: Cal: 70, Protein: 2g, Carbs: 15g, Fat: 0.5g, Sodium: 20mg, Fiber: 2g

Chocolate Avocado Ice Cream

PREP: 15 mins
Cook T.: 4 hrs (freezing)
Serves: 4
Ingr:
- 1 ripe avocado
- 1/4 C unsweetened cocoa powder
- 1/4 C honey
- 1 tsp vanilla extract
- 1/2 C almond milk

Proc:
1. Blend all ingredients until creamy.
2. Pour into a container and freeze for 4 hrs.
3. Scoop and serve.

Nutritional Values: Cal: 180, Protein: 2g, Carbs: 28g, Fat: 8g, Sodium: 10mg, Fiber: 6g

Peach Ginger Sorbet

PREP: 10 mins
Cook T.: 4 hrs (freezing)
Serves: 4
Ingr:
- 3 ripe peaches
- 1 tbsp fresh ginger, grated
- 2 tbsp honey
- 1 tsp lemon juice
- A pinch of salt

Proc:
1. Blend all ingredients until smooth.
2. Pour into a container and freeze for 4 hrs.
3. Scoop and serve.

Nutritional Values: Cal: 80, Protein: 1g, Carbs: 20g, Fat: 0.5g, Sodium: 10mg, Fiber: 2g

Coconut Lime Popsicles

PREP: 10 mins
Cook T.: 6 hrs (freezing)
Serves: 6
Ingr:
- 1 can (13.5 oz) light coconut milk
- Zest and juice of 1 lime
- 3 tbsp honey
- A pinch of salt

Proc:
1. Mix all ingredients until well combined.
2. Pour into popsicle molds and insert sticks.
3. Freeze for 6 hrs or until set.

Nutritional Values: Cal: 90, Protein: 1g, Carbs: 12g, Fat: 5g, Sodium: 15mg, Fiber: 0g

Watermelon Mint Granita

PREP: 15 mins
Cook T.: 4 hrs (freezing and scraping)
Serves: 4
Ingr:
- 4 Cs watermelon cubes
- 10 mint leaves
- 2 tbsp honey
- 1 tsp lime juice

Proc:
1. Blend watermelon, mint, honey, and lime juice until smooth.
2. Pour into a shallow dish and freeze for 1 hour.
3. Scrape with a fork every 30 mins for the next 3 hrs.
4. Serve in bowls.

Nutritional Values: Cal: 60, Protein: 1g, Carbs: 15g, Fat: 0.5g, Sodium: 5mg, Fiber: 1g

Pineapple Coconut Sorbet

PREP: 10 mins
Cook T.: 4 hrs (freezing)
Serves: 4
Ingr:
- 2 Cs pineapple chunks
- 1/2 C light coconut milk
- 2 tbsp honey
- A pinch of salt

Proc:
1. Blend all ingredients until smooth.
2. Pour into a container and freeze for 4 hrs.
3. Scoop and serve.

Nutritional Values: Cal: 90, Protein: 1g, Carbs: 20g, Fat: 2g, Sodium: 10mg, Fiber: 1g

Banana Chocolate Popsicles

PREP: 10 mins
Cook T.: 6 hrs (freezing)
Serves: 6
Ingr:
- 3 ripe bananas
- 1/4 C unsweetened cocoa powder
- 1/4 C almond milk
- 2 tbsp honey

Proc:

1. Blend all ingredients until creamy.
2. Pour into popsicle molds and insert sticks.
3. Freeze for 6 hrs or until set.

Nutritional Values: Cal: 90, Protein: 2g, Carbs: 22g, Fat: 1g, Sodium: 5mg, Fiber: 3g

Strawberry Basil Sorbet

PREP: 10 mins
Cook T.: 4 hrs (freezing)
Serves: 4
Ingr:
- 2 Cs strawberries
- 10 basil leaves
- 2 tbsp honey
- 1 tsp lemon juice

Proc:

1. Blend all ingredients until smooth.
2. Pour into a container and freeze for 4 hrs.
3. Scoop and serve.

Nutritional Values: Cal: 60, Protein: 1g, Carbs: 15g, Fat: 0.5g, Sodium: 5mg, Fiber: 2g

Kiwi Lime Granita

PREP: 15 mins
Cook T.: 4 hrs (freezing and scraping)
Serves: 4
Ingr:
- 4 kiwis, peeled
- Zest and juice of 1 lime
- 2 tbsp honey

Proc:

1. Blend kiwi, lime zest, lime juice, and honey until smooth.
2. Pour into a shallow dish and freeze for 1 hour.
3. Scrape with a fork every 30 mins for the next 3 hrs.
4. Serve in bowls.

Nutritional Values: Cal: 70, Protein: 1g, Carbs: 18g, Fat: 0.5g, Sodium: 5mg, Fiber: 3g

Cherry Almond Ice Cream

PREP: 15 mins
Cook T.: 4 hrs (freezing)
Serves: 4
Ingr:
- 2 Cs cherries, pitted
- 1/2 C almond milk
- 2 tbsp honey
- 1 tsp almond extract

Proc:
1. Blend cherries, almond milk, honey, and almond extract until creamy.
2. Pour into a container and freeze for 4 hrs.
3. Scoop and serve.

Nutritional Values: Cal: 80, Protein: 1g, Carbs: 18g, Fat: 1g, Sodium: 10mg, Fiber: 2g

Chapter 8: Special Recipes

Slow Cooker Dishes

Chicken And Vegetables

PREP: 15 mins
Cook T.: 6 hrs
Serves: 4
Ingr:

- 4 boneless chicken breasts
- 2 Cs mixed vegetables (carrots, green beans, bell peppers)
- 1 C low-sodium chicken broth
- 1 tsp dried thyme
- 1 tsp garlic powder

Proc:

1. Place chicken breasts at the bottom of the slow cooker.
2. Add mixed vegetables on top.
3. Pour chicken broth and sprinkle thyme and garlic powder.
4. Cover and cook on low for 6 hrs.
5. Serve warm.

Nutritional Values: Cal: 220, Protein: 28g, Carbs: 10g, Fat: 6g, Sodium: 120mg, Fiber: 3g

Slow Cooker Lentil Soup

PREP: 10 mins
Cook T.: 8 hrs
Serves: 6
Ingr:

- 1 C dried lentils
- 4 Cs low-sodium vegetable broth
- 2 carrots, sliced
- 1 onion, chpd
- 2 garlic cloves, minced

Proc:

1. Combine all ingredients in the slow cooker.
2. Cover and cook on low for 8 hrs.
3. Stir well before serving.

Nutritional Values: Cal: 180, Protein: 12g, Carbs: 30g, Fat: 0.5g, Sodium: 70mg, Fiber: 8g

Turkey Chili

PREP: 15 mins
Cook T.: 6 hrs
Serves: 4
Ingr:

- 1 lb ground turkey
- 1 can (15 oz) low-sodium diced tomatoes
- 1 can (15 oz) low-sodium black beans, drained
- 1 onion, chpd
- 2 tbsp chili powder

Proc:

1. Brown turkey in a skillet and transfer to the slow cooker.
2. Add the rest of the ingredients.
3. Cover and cook on low for 6 hrs.
4. Stir well before serving.

Nutritional Values: Cal: 320, Protein: 28g, Carbs: 35g, Fat: 8g, Sodium: 200mg, Fiber: 10g

Spinach And Feta Stuffed Chicken

PREP: 20 mins
Cook T.: 5 hrs
Serves: 4
Ingr:
- 4 boneless chicken breasts
- 1 C fresh spinach, chpd
- 1/2 C feta cheese, crumbled
- 1 tsp garlic powder
- 1 C low-sodium chicken broth

Proc:

1. Make a pocket in each chicken breast and stuff with spinach and feta.
2. Place in the slow cooker and sprinkle with garlic powder.
3. Pour chicken broth over the chicken.
4. Cover and cook on low for 5 hrs.
5. Serve warm.

Nutritional Values: Cal: 240, Protein: 30g, Carbs: 3g, Fat: 10g, Sodium: 220mg, Fiber: 1g

Vegetable Curry

PREP: 15 mins
Cook T.: 6 hrs
Serves: 4
Ingr:
- 2 Cs cauliflower florets
- 1 bell pepper, sliced
- 1 can (15 oz) low-sodium chickpeas, drained
- 1 can (13.5 oz) light coconut milk
- 2 tbsp curry powder

Proc:
1. Combine all ingredients in the slow cooker.
2. Cover and cook on low for 6 hrs.
3. Stir well before serving.

Nutritional Values: Cal: 220, Protein: 8g, Carbs: 25g, Fat: 10g, Sodium: 150mg, Fiber: 7g

Beef And Broccoli

PREP: 15 mins
Cook T.: 6 hrs
Serves: 4
Ingr:
- 1 lb beef slices
- 2 Cs broccoli florets
- 1/2 C low-sodium soy sauce
- 2 garlic cloves, minced
- 1 tbsp honey

Proc:
1. Place beef slices at the bottom of the slow cooker.
2. In a bowl, mix soy sauce, garlic, and honey, then pour over the beef.
3. Cover and cook on low for 5 hrs.
4. Add broccoli and cook for an additional hour.
5. Serve warm.

Nutritional Values: Cal: 280, Protein: 28g, Carbs: 15g, Fat: 12g, Sodium: 400mg, Fiber: 2g

Quinoa And Vegetable Stew

PREP: 10 mins
Cook T.: 6 hrs
Serves: 4
Ingr:

- 1 C quinoa, rinsed
- 4 Cs low-sodium vegetable broth
- 2 zucchinis, sliced
- 1 bell pepper, chpd
- 1 tsp dried basil

Proc:

1. Combine all ingredients in the slow cooker.
2. Cover and cook on low for 6 hrs.
3. Stir well before serving.

Nutritional Values: Cal: 220, Protein: 8g, Carbs: 40g, Fat: 3g, Sodium: 150mg, Fiber: 5g

Tuscan Chicken

PREP: 15 mins
Cook T.: 6 hrs
Serves: 4
Ingr:

- 4 boneless chicken breasts
- 1 can (15 oz) low-sodium diced tomatoes
- 1/2 C sun-dried tomatoes, chpd
- 1/4 C black olives, sliced
- 1 tsp dried oregano

Proc:

1. Place chicken breasts at the bottom of the slow cooker.
2. Add the rest of the ingredients on top.
3. Cover and cook on low for 6 hrs.
4. Serve warm.

Nutritional Values: Cal: 230, Protein: 28g, Carbs: 15g, Fat: 6g, Sodium: 220mg, Fiber: 3g

Pumpkin Soup

PREP: 10 mins
Cook T.: 6 hrs
Serves: 6
Ingr:

- 2 Cs pumpkin puree
- 4 Cs low-sodium vegetable broth
- 1 onion, chpd
- 2 garlic cloves, minced
- 1 tsp ground cinnamon

Proc:

1. Combine all ingredients in the slow cooker.
2. Cover and cook on low for 6 hrs.
3. Blend until smooth before serving.

Nutritional Values: Cal: 70, Protein: 2g, Carbs: 15g, Fat: 0.5g, Sodium: 70mg, Fiber: 3g

Garlic Herb Mushrooms

PREP: 10 mins
Cook T.: 4 hrs
Serves: 4
Ingr:

- 1 lb mushrooms, cleaned
- 1/4 C low-sodium vegetable broth
- 3 garlic cloves, minced
- 1 tsp dried rosemary
- 1 tsp dried thyme

Proc:
1. Combine all ingredients in the slow cooker.
2. Cover and cook on low for 4 hrs.

3. Stir well before serving.

Nutritional Values: Cal: 50, Protein: 4g, Carbs: 7g, Fat: 0.5g, Sodium: 50mg, Fiber: 2g

Spaghetti Squash And Meatballs

PREP: 20 mins
Cook T.: 5 hrs
Serves: 4
Ingr:
- 1 spaghetti squash, halved and seeds removed
- 12 turkey meatballs
- 1 can (15 oz) low-sodium tomato sauce
- 1 onion, chpd
- 2 garlic cloves, minced

Proc:
1. Place spaghetti squash halves face down in the slow cooker.
2. Add meatballs, tomato sauce, onion, and garlic.
3. Cover and cook on low for 5 hrs.
4. Use a fork to shred the spaghetti squash and mix with the sauce and meatballs before serving.

Nutritional Values: Cal: 280, Protein: 20g, Carbs: 30g, Fat: 8g, Sodium: 220mg, Fiber: 6g

Mediterranean Dishes

Mediterranean Chickpea Salad

PREP: 15 mins
Cook T.: 0 mins
Serves: 4
Ingr:
- 1 can (15 oz) low-sodium chickpeas, drained and rinsed
- 1 cucumber, diced
- 1 bell pepper, diced
- 1/4 C feta cheese, crumbled
- 2 tbsp olive oil

Proc:
1. In a large bowl, combine chickpeas, cucumber, and bell pepper.
2. Drizzle with olive oil and toss to coat.
3. Sprinkle with feta cheese.
4. Chill for 30 mins before serving.
5. Enjoy as a refreshing side dish.

Nutritional Values: Cal: 220, Protein: 8g, Carbs: 25g, Fat: 10g, Sodium: 150mg, Fiber: 6g

Stuffed Tomatoes

PREP: 20 mins
Cook T.: 25 mins
Serves: 4
Ingr:
- 4 large tomatoes
- 1 C cooked quinoa
- 1/4 C black olives, chpd
- 1/4 C fresh basil, chpd
- 2 tbsp olive oil

Proc:
1. Preheat oven to 375°F (190°C).
2. Cut off the tops of the tomatoes and scoop out the insides.
3. In a bowl, mix quinoa, olives, basil, and olive oil.
4. Stuff each tomato with the quinoa mixture.
5. Place in a baking dish and bake for 25 mins.

Nutritional Values: Cal: 180, Protein: 4g, Carbs: 20g, Fat: 10g, Sodium: 100mg, Fiber: 4g

Mediterranean Lemon Herb Chicken

PREP: 10 mins
Cook T.: 25 mins
Serves: 4
Ingr:
- 4 boneless chicken breasts
- 2 lemons, juiced
- 2 garlic cloves, minced
- 1 tsp dried oregano
- 2 tbsp olive oil

Proc:
1. In a bowl, mix lemon juice, garlic, oregano, and olive oil.
2. Marinate chicken in the mixture for at least 30 mins.
3. Preheat grill or skillet over medium heat.
4. Cook chicken for 12-15 mins on each side or until done.

5. Serve with a side of steamed vegetables.

Nutritional Values: Cal: 240, Protein: 28g, Carbs: 5g, Fat: 12g, Sodium: 70mg, Fiber: 1g

Eggplant Dip

PREP: 10 mins
Cook T.: 40 mins
Serves: 6
Ingr:
- 1 large eggplant
- 2 garlic cloves, minced
- 2 tbsp tahini
- 1 lemon, juiced
- 1 tbsp olive oil

Proc:
1. Preheat oven to 400°F (200°C).
2. Prick eggplant with a fork and place on a baking sheet.
3. Roast for 40 mins or until soft.
4. Let cool, then peel and place in a blender.
5. Add garlic, tahini, lemon juice, and olive oil. Blend until smooth.

Nutritional Values: Cal: 90, Protein: 2g, Carbs: 10g, Fat: 5g, Sodium: 20mg, Fiber: 4g

Fish Stew

PREP: 15 mins
Cook T.: 30 mins
Serves: 4
Ingr:
- 1 lb white fish fillets, cut into chunks
- 1 can (15 oz) low-sodium diced tomatoes
- 1 onion, chpd
- 2 garlic cloves, minced
- 1/4 C fresh parsley, chpd

Proc:
1. In a pot, sauté onion and garlic until translucent.
2. Add tomatoes and bring to a simmer.
3. Add fish chunks and cook until fish is done, about 10 mins.
4. Garnish with fresh parsley before serving.

Nutritional Values: Cal: 180, Protein: 25g, Carbs: 10g, Fat: 3g, Sodium: 100mg, Fiber: 2g

Spinach And Feta Pasta

PREP: 10 mins
Cook T.: 20 mins
Serves: 4
Ingr:
- 8 oz whole wheat spaghetti
- 2 Cs fresh spinach, chpd
- 1/4 C feta cheese, crumbled
- 2 garlic cloves, minced
- 2 tbsp olive oil

Proc:
1. Cook spaghetti according to package instructions.
2. In a skillet, sauté garlic in olive oil until fragrant.
3. Add spinach and cook until wilted.
4. Toss cooked spaghetti with spinach mixture.
5. Top with feta cheese before serving.

Nutritional Values: Cal: 280, Protein: 10g, Carbs: 40g, Fat: 10g, Sodium: 150mg, Fiber: 6g

Lentil Salad

PREP: 15 mins
Cook T.: 25 mins
Serves: 4
Ingr:
- 1 C dried lentils
- 1 cucumber, diced
- 1 bell pepper, diced
- 1/4 C fresh mint, chpd
- 2 tbsp olive oil

Proc:
1. Cook lentils according to package instructions.
2. In a large bowl, combine cooked lentils, cucumber, bell pepper, and mint.
3. Drizzle with olive oil and toss to combine.
4. Chill for at least 1 hour before serving.

Nutritional Values: Cal: 220, Protein: 12g, Carbs: 30g, Fat: 7g, Sodium: 10mg, Fiber: 8g

Olive Tapenade

PREP: 10 mins
Cook T.: 0 mins
Serves: 6
Ingr:
- 1 C green olives, pitted
- 1 C black olives, pitted
- 2 garlic cloves
- 1 lemon, juiced
- 2 tbsp olive oil

Proc:
1. Combine all ingredients in a food processor.
2. Blend until smooth.
3. Serve with whole wheat crackers or sliced cucumber.

Nutritional Values: Cal: 120, Protein: 1g, Carbs: 3g, Fat: 12g, Sodium: 300mg, Fiber: 1g

Zucchini Boats

PREP: 15 mins
Cook T.: 25 mins
Serves: 4
Ingr:
- 2 large zucchinis, halved lengthwise
- 1 C cooked quinoa
- 1/4 C sun-dried tomatoes, chpd
- 1/4 C feta cheese, crumbled
- 2 tbsp olive oil

Proc:
1. Preheat oven to 375°F (190°C).
2. Scoop out the insides of the zucchinis to create a boat.
3. In a bowl, mix quinoa, sun-dried tomatoes, feta, and olive oil.
4. Stuff zucchini halves with the mixture.
5. Place in a baking dish and bake for 25 mins.

Nutritional Values: Cal: 180, Protein: 6g, Carbs: 20g, Fat: 10g, Sodium: 150mg, Fiber: 3g

Bean Soup

PREP: 10 mins
Cook T.: 30 mins
Serves: 4
Ingr:
- 1 can (15 oz) low-sodium white beans, drained and rinsed
- 1 can (15 oz) low-sodium diced tomatoes
- 1 onion, chpd
- 2 garlic cloves, minced
- 2 tbsp olive oil

Proc:
1. In a pot, sauté onion and garlic in olive oil until translucent.
2. Add beans, tomatoes, and 4 Cs of water.
3. Bring to a boil, then reduce heat and simmer for 30 mins.
4. Serve with a sprinkle of fresh parsley.

Nutritional Values: Cal: 220, Protein: 8g, Carbs: 30g, Fat: 7g, Sodium: 100mg, Fiber: 8g

Mediterranean Roasted Vegetables

PREP: 15 mins
Cook T.: 25 mins
Serves: 4
Ingr:
- 2 bell peppers, sliced
- 1 zucchini, sliced
- 1 eggplant, sliced
- 2 tbsp olive oil
- 1 tsp dried oregano

Proc:
1. Preheat oven to 400°F (200°C).
2. Toss vegetables with olive oil and oregano.
3. Spread on a baking sheet in a single layer.
4. Roast for 25 mins or until tender.

Nutritional Values: Cal: 120, Protein: 2g, Carbs: 15g, Fat: 7g, Sodium: 10mg, Fiber: 5g

Artichoke Dip

PREP: 10 mins
Cook T.: 0 mins
Serves: 6
Ingr:
- 1 can (14 oz) artichoke hearts, drained and chpd
- 1/4 C Greek yogurt
- 1 garlic clove, minced
- 1 lemon, juiced
- 2 tbsp olive oil

Proc:
1. In a food processor, combine artichoke hearts, Greek yogurt, garlic, and lemon juice.
2. Blend until smooth.
3. While blending, slowly drizzle in the olive oil until well combined.
4. Transfer to a serving bowl and chill for at least 1 hour before serving.
5. Enjoy with whole wheat crackers or sliced cucumber.

Nutritional Values: Cal: 90, Protein: 2g, Carbs: 5g, Fat: 7g, Sodium: 60mg, Fiber: 2g

Stuffed Peppers

PREP: 20 mins
Cook T.: 30 mins
Serves: 4
Ingr:
- 4 bell peppers, tops removed and seeds scooped out
- 1 C cooked bulgur wheat
- 1/4 C black olives, chpd
- 1/4 C feta cheese, crumbled
- 2 tbsp olive oil

Proc:
1. Preheat oven to 375°F (190°C).
2. In a bowl, mix bulgur wheat, olives, feta cheese, and olive oil.
3. Stuff each bell pepper with the bulgur mixture.
4. Place the stuffed peppers in a baking dish.
5. Cover with aluminum foil and bake for 30 mins or until peppers are tender.

Nutritional Values: Cal: 220, Protein: 6g, Carbs: 25g, Fat: 12g, Sodium: 150mg, Fiber: 6g

SCAN QR CODE TO DOWNLOAD EXTRA CONTENT

Chapter 9: Meal planning for 28 days

Week 1 Meal Plan

Day	Breakfast	Lunch	Dinner	Snack	Dessert
1	Quinoa and Berry Breakfast Bowl	Mediterranean Chickpea Salad	Grilled Lemon Herb Chicken	Roasted Red Pepper Hummus	Berry Medley Parfait
2	Oatmeal with Cinnamon and Apple	Spinach and Strawberry Salad	Baked Salmon with Dill and Lemon	Avocado And Cilantro Dip	Citrus Fruit Salad
3	Millet Porridge with Banana	Quinoa and Avocado Bowl	Herb-Crusted Tilapia	Sun-Dried Tomato Spread	Baked Apples With Cinnamon
4	Barley and Nut Breakfast Pudding	Roasted Beet and Arugula Salad	Spiced Turkey Patties	Lemon And Herb Yogurt Dip	Mango Sorbet
5	Rye Flakes and Dried Fruit Compote	Tuna and White Bean Salad	Lemon Pepper Shrimp Skewers	Balsamic Fig And Ricotta Spread	Banana And Berry Smoothie Bowl
6	Buckwheat and Berry Morning Delight	Asian-inspired Broccoli and Almond Salad	Rosemary Lamb Chops	Spicy Black Bean Dip	Grilled Pineapple Slices
7	Whole Wheat Berry Pancakes	Grilled Chicken and Mango Salad	Tofu Steak with Ginger Soy Glaze	Roasted Garlic And White Bean Dip	Strawberry And Kiwi Tart

Week 1 Shopping List
Proteins: Chicken breasts, Salmon fillets, Tilapia fillets, Turkey, Shrimp, Lamb chops, Tofu.
Grains: Quinoa, Rolled oats, Millet, Barley, Rye flakes, Buckwheat, Whole wheat flour for pancakes.
Vegetables/Fruits: Mixed berries (strawberries, blueberries, raspberries), Apples, Bananas, Beets, Arugula, Spinach, Lemons, Avocado, Red bell peppers, Cucumber, Mango, Broccoli, White beans, Almonds, Pineapple, Kiwi, Eggplant, Tomatoes, Olives, Artichokes.
Dairy & Alternatives: Greek yogurt, Feta cheese, Ricotta cheese.

Herbs & Spices: Cinnamon, Dill, Rosemary, Ginger, Garlic, Basil, Parsley, Mint.
Miscellaneous: Olive oil, Balsamic vinegar, Sun-dried tomatoes, Hummus, Black beans, White beans, Chickpeas, Lentils.

Week 2 Meal Plan

Day	Breakfast	Lunch	Dinner	Snack	Dessert
1	Millet Porridge with Banana	Tuna and Cucumber Sandwich	Herb-Crusted Tilapia	Roasted Chickpea Crunch	Mango Sorbet
2	Barley and Nut Breakfast Pudding	Grilled Chicken and Avocado Wrap	Spiced Turkey Patties	Baked Kale Chips	Peach and Raspberry Crumble
3	Rye Flakes and Dried Fruit Compote	Asian-inspired Broccoli and Almond Salad	Balsamic Glazed Chicken Thighs	Spicy Roasted Almonds	Strawberry and Kiwi Tart
4	Buckwheat and Berry Morning Delight	Turkey and Cranberry Wrap	Lemon Pepper Shrimp Skewers	Crispy Edamame	Blueberry Lavender Smoothie
5	Whole Wheat Berry Pancakes	Mediterranean Veggie Wrap	Seared Cod with Lemon-Parsley Drizzle	Roasted Pumpkin Seeds	Chocolate Zucchini Muffins
6	Cornmeal and Apple Porridge	Spicy Tofu Sandwich	Spiced Beef Kebabs	Baked Zucchini Chips	Banana and Coconut Muffins
7	Spelt and Nut Muesli	Smoked Salmon and Cream Cheese Wrap	Tofu Steak with Ginger Soy Glaze	Crispy Brussels Sprout Chips	Vanilla and Berry Cake

Week 2 Shopping List
Proteins: Chicken breasts, Salmon fillets, Tilapia fillets, Turkey, Shrimp, Beef, Tofu.
Grains: Millet, Barley, Rye flakes, Buckwheat, Whole wheat flour for pancakes, Cornmeal, Spelt.
Vegetables/Fruits: Bananas, Mixed berries (strawberries, blueberries, raspberries), Apples, Broccoli, Avocado, Lemons, Cucumber, Mango, Kiwi, Eggplant, Tomatoes, Olives, Artichokes, Zucchini, Brussels sprouts.
Dairy & Alternatives: Greek yogurt, Cream cheese, Coconut for muffins.
Herbs & Spices: Cinnamon, Dill, Ginger, Garlic, Basil, Parsley, Rosemary, Soy sauce.
Miscellaneous: Olive oil, Balsamic vinegar, Sun-dried tomatoes, Hummus, Black beans, White beans, Chickpeas, Lentils.

Adjust quantities as needed based on the number of servings you plan to prepare.

Week 3 Meal Plan

Day	Breakfast	Lunch	Dinner	Snack	Dessert
1	Amaranth and Coconut Bowl	Roasted Vegetable and Hummus Sandwich	Rosemary Lamb Chops	Crispy Cauliflower Bites	Grilled Pineapple Slices
2	Sorghum and Date Pudding	Egg Salad and Spinach Wrap	Spicy Grilled Tempeh	Roasted Sweet Potato Wedges	Melon Ball Salad
3	Teff and Cinnamon Porridge	Chicken Caesar Salad Wrap	Tomato Lentil Stew	Crunchy Green Pea Snack	Tropical Fruit Popsicles
4	Quinoa and Berry Breakfast Bowl	Roast Beef and Horseradish Sandwich	Creamy Coconut Chickpea Curry	Baked Zucchini Chips	Lemon and Poppy Seed Muffins
5	Oatmeal with Cinnamon and Apple	Veggie and Pesto Wrap	Vegetable Quinoa Stew	Crispy Brussels Sprout Chips	Cinnamon Apple Cake
6	Millet Porridge with Banana	Grilled Chicken and Avocado Wrap	Mushroom Barley Soup	Roasted Chickpea Crunch	Blueberry Oat Muffins
7	Barley and Nut Breakfast Pudding	Tuna and Cucumber Sandwich	Sweet Potato and Coconut Soup	Baked Kale Chips	Chocolate and Orange Cake

Week 3 Shopping List
Proteins: Chicken breasts, Lamb chops, Tempeh, Beef, Tuna.
Grains: Amaranth, Sorghum, Teff, Quinoa, Oatmeal, Barley, Millet.
Vegetables/Fruits: Coconut, Dates, Berries (strawberries, blueberries), Apples, Mixed vegetables for roasting (bell peppers, zucchini, eggplant), Spinach, Tomatoes, Lentils, Chickpeas, Mushrooms, Sweet potatoes, Pineapple, Melon.
Dairy & Alternatives: Greek yogurt, Horseradish sauce, Hummus, Caesar dressing, Pesto.
Herbs & Spices: Cinnamon, Rosemary, Ginger, Garlic, Basil, Parsley, Lemon.
Miscellaneous: Olive oil, Balsamic vinegar, Sun-dried tomatoes, Black beans, White beans, Almonds.

Week 4 Meal Plan

Day	Breakfast	Lunch	Dinner	Snack	Dessert
1	Buckwheat and Berry Morning Delight	Mediterranean Veggie Wrap	Spiced Beef Kebabs	Crispy Edamame	Strawberry And Kiwi Tart
2	Cornmeal and Apple Porridge	Smoked Salmon and Cream Cheese Wrap	Fish and Spinach Curry	Roasted Pumpkin Seeds	Peach And Raspberry Crumble
3	Spelt and Nut Muesli	Turkey and Cranberry Wrap	Beef and Tomato Stew	Baked Zucchini Chips	Vanilla And Berry Cake
4	Whole Wheat Berry Pancakes	Grilled Portobello and Pesto Sandwich	Brown Rice Pilaf with Almonds	Spicy Roasted Cashews	Banana And Coconut Muffins
5	Rye Flakes and Dried Fruit Compote	Roasted Vegetable and Hummus Sandwich	Farro with Roasted Vegetables	Crunchy Beet Chips	Chocolate Zucchini Muffins
6	Barley and Nut Breakfast Pudding	Tuna and Cucumber Sandwich	Bulgur Wheat with Lemon and Parsley	Crispy Brussels Sprout Chips	Carrot And Walnut Cake
7	Millet Porridge with Banana	Grilled Chicken and Avocado Wrap	Rye Berries with Roasted Beets and Goat Cheese	Roasted Sweet Potato Wedges	Raspberry Coconut Muffins

Week 4 Shopping List

Proteins: Beef, Fish, Turkey, Smoked Salmon, Chicken breasts.

Grains: Buckwheat, Cornmeal, Spelt, Whole Wheat, Rye Flakes, Barley, Brown Rice, Farro, Bulgur Wheat, Rye Berries.

Vegetables/Fruits: Berries (strawberries, blueberries, raspberries), Apples, Portobello mushrooms, Spinach, Tomatoes, Beets, Goat Cheese, Kiwi, Peach, Banana, Zucchini, Carrot, Walnut, Coconut.

Dairy & Alternatives: Cream Cheese, Greek yogurt, Hummus, Pesto.

Herbs & Spices: Dried fruits (raisins, apricots), Lemon, Parsley, Cranberry sauce, Garlic, Basil.

Miscellaneous: Olive oil, Balsamic vinegar, Sun-dried tomatoes, Pumpkin seeds, Cashews.

Conclusion

Final Reflections

As we come to the end of this comprehensive guide, it's essential to pause and reflect on the journey we've embarked upon together. The DASH Diet, while rooted in scientific principles and health benefits, is more than just a dietary regimen. It's a lifestyle, a commitment, and a testament to the belief that our health is in our hands.

The Power of Choice

Every meal we've discussed, every recipe we've explored, underscores one fundamental principle: the power of choice. We live in a world inundated with fast food options, processed meals, and quick fixes. Yet, with the DASH Diet, we've chosen a different path. We've chosen health over convenience, longevity over momentary pleasure, and knowledge over ignorance. This choice is empowering. It's a declaration that we value ourselves, our health, and the health of our loved ones.

The Beauty of Simplicity

One of the most striking aspects of the DASH Diet is its simplicity. There's no need for fancy ingredients, complicated procedures, or expensive supplements. The diet emphasizes whole foods, natural ingredients, and the beauty of home-cooked meals. This simplicity is a reminder that often, in our quest for health, we don't need to look for the next big thing or the latest fad. Nature, in its infinite wisdom, has provided us with everything we need. Our job is to make choices that align with this natural bounty.

The Ripple Effect

While the primary focus of the DASH Diet is on individual health, it's essential to recognize the broader impact of our choices. When we choose fresh over processed, homemade over store-bought, and natural over artificial, we're not just improving our health. We're supporting local farmers, promoting sustainable agriculture, and reducing our carbon footprint. Our choices have a ripple effect, touching lives and systems far beyond our immediate circle. This interconnectedness is a beautiful reminder that our health and the health of our planet are inextricably linked.

The Transformative Power of Knowledge

Knowledge, they say, is power. But knowledge without application is like a lamp kept under a basket. Throughout this guide, we've armed you with knowledge. We've delved into the science behind the DASH Diet, explored its myriad benefits, and provided practical tools to integrate it into your life. But the real transformation happens when you apply this knowledge. Every time you choose a DASH-approved meal, every time you opt for a healthier alternative, you're applying this knowledge. And with each application, you're transforming your life, one meal at a time.

Embracing the Journey

It's essential to remember that adopting the DASH Diet is not about perfection. It's about progress. There will be days when you slip up, moments when you give in to temptation. And that's okay. What's important is not the occasional misstep but the overall journey. It's about getting up each time you fall, learning from your mistakes, and moving forward with renewed commitment. The DASH Diet is not a destination; it's a journey. And like all journeys, it's the experiences, the learnings, and the memories that make it worthwhile.

How to Maintain a DASH Approach in Everyday Life

One of the foundational pillars of the DASH approach is mindfulness. It's about being present in the moment, being aware of our choices, and understanding their implications. This mindfulness extends beyond our meals. It's about cultivating an awareness of our body, understanding its signals, and responding with care and compassion. By practicing mindfulness, we can ensure that our commitment to the DASH approach remains unwavering, even in the face of challenges.

Building a Supportive Community

Humans are inherently social beings. We thrive in communities, drawing strength, inspiration, and support from those around us. To maintain a DASH approach in everyday life, it's crucial to surround ourselves with like-minded individuals. Whether it's joining a DASH Diet support group, participating in community cooking classes, or simply sharing your journey with friends and family, building a supportive community can be a game-changer.

Embracing Flexibility

While the DASH Diet provides guidelines and principles, it's essential to remember that life is unpredictable. There will be days when you can't stick to the plan, occasions when indulgence takes precedence, and moments when life gets in the way. And that's perfectly okay. The key is to embrace flexibility. Instead of beating yourself up over deviations, use them as learning opportunities. Understand what triggered the deviation, learn from it, and move forward with renewed commitment.

Continuous Learning

The world of nutrition is dynamic, with new research and findings emerging regularly. To maintain a DASH approach in everyday life, it's essential to stay updated. Whether it's subscribing to a health magazine, attending workshops, or simply engaging in conversations with nutritionists, continuous learning ensures that your approach to the DASH Diet remains relevant, informed, and effective.

Celebrating Small Wins

Every meal where you choose health over convenience, every day you stick to the

DASH principles, and every milestone you achieve, no matter how small, is a win. And it's essential to celebrate these wins. By acknowledging and celebrating your achievements, you reinforce positive behavior, boost your motivation, and strengthen your commitment to the DASH approach.

Integrating DASH into Daily Rituals

The DASH approach isn't just about meals; it's a way of life. By integrating DASH principles into daily rituals, you ensure that it becomes second nature. Whether it's starting your day with a DASH-approved smoothie, incorporating DASH-friendly snacks into your work routine, or ending your day with a DASH-compliant dessert, integrating DASH into daily rituals ensures consistency and commitment.

Appendix Further Reading and Additional Resources

Books to Enhance Your DASH Knowledge

1. **"The DASH Diet Action Plan"** by Marla Heller: A comprehensive guide that offers practical tips, meal plans, and recipes to help you embrace the DASH lifestyle seamlessly.
2. **"The Salt Solution"** by Heather K. Jones and the Editors of Prevention: This book delves deep into the impact of salt on our health and offers actionable strategies to reduce sodium intake.
3. **"Mindful Eating"** by Jan Chozen Bays: While not exclusively about DASH, this book provides insights into the practice of mindful eating, which can enhance your adherence to the DASH principles.

Websites and Online Platforms

1. **The National Heart, Lung, and Blood Institute (NHLBI)**: The NHLBI offers a plethora of resources on the DASH diet, including meal plans, shopping lists, and more.
2. **MyFitnessPal**: This popular app can help you track your sodium intake, ensuring you stay within the DASH recommended limits.

3. **DASH Diet Collection at EatingWell**: A treasure trove of DASH-compliant recipes, meal plans, and tips to make your DASH journey delicious and varied.

Podcasts and Webinars
1. **"Nutrition Diva"** by Monica Reinagel: While it covers a broad range of nutrition topics, several episodes delve into the principles aligned with the DASH diet.
2. **"The Salt Solution & High Blood Pressure"** Webinar: An insightful webinar that explores the link between sodium and hypertension, reinforcing the principles of the DASH diet.

Workshops and Classes
1. **Local Community Centers**: Many community centers offer nutrition workshops that touch upon the principles of the DASH diet.
2. **Cooking Schools**: Look for classes that focus on heart-healthy or low-sodium cooking. These often align with DASH principles and can offer hands-on experience in preparing DASH-compliant meals.

Support Groups and Communities
1. **DASH Diet Facebook Group**: A vibrant community where members share recipes, success stories, challenges, and tips related to the DASH diet.
2. **Local Support Groups**: Check local listings or community boards for DASH diet or low-sodium support groups where you can connect with like-minded individuals.

Made in the USA
Columbia, SC
23 September 2024

42784482R00059